"You have used great wisdom and have p[...] people] to give glory to the Lord....God has given you a significant role in these Vanuatans' lives. I know their future is now brighter....I know that you have been wonderfully used by Him."

—*Dr. Loren Cunningham, founder and chairman of Youth With A Mission*

"John Rush has discovered still another example of a gospel precursor hidden within the culture of an unreached people group. Like the examples I documented in *Eternity in Their Hearts,* this precursor also helped to open the eyes of people who need Jesus. John's moving adventure brings us one frontier closer to the reaching of the last tribe!"

—*Don Richardson, author of best-sellers* Peace Child, Lords of the Earth, *and* Eternity in Their Hearts

"*The Man with the Bird on His Head* is a fascinating true story about God's providential guidance, an unusual cargo cult in the South Pacific waiting for the Messiah named "John Frum," and the faith of "John from" America who God used to touch a whole tribe with the Gospel. I was mesmerized as I experienced John Rush tell his story."

—*Dr. Linus Morris, author and Executive Director, Christian Associates International*

"A well-written and exciting adventure of how God prepared the hearts of these Pacific Island people for the gospel and how He prepared a messenger to be the bearer of the good news. A great book to stimulate interest in missions because it portrays God's providence so vividly."

—*Dr. Arthur G. Patzia, author and Director/Associate Professor of New Testament, Fuller Seminary in Northern California*

"This is a remarkable story about an unreached people group in the South Pacific prepared and waiting for the arrival of one man on a white Mercy Ship."

—*Don Stephens, President and CEO, Mercy Ships*

"It is good news that you and Abbe are bringing this testimony into being. I am sure it will be an inspiration to others to the glory of our God."

—*Professor Herbert Ford, Director Pitcairn Islands Study Center, Pacific Union College*

"One of the most amazing missionary stories of the twentieth century! Highly recommended!"

—*Diana Waring, Homeschool leader and author of* Things We Wish We'd Known

"My family and I have been on Tanna Island since 1991. I really enjoyed reading *The Man with the Bird on His Head.* I could picture things clearly not only because the book was really well written but also because we know many of the people and places you mentioned. I think the Lord really did open up those special contacts with the John Frum people for you.... I see that God used you in a very particular way to challenge Isaac Wan and draw him and his people closer to the Lord."

—*Greg Carlson, Wycliffe Bible translator*

THE MAN WITH THE BIRD ON HIS HEAD

The Amazing Fulfillment of
a Mysterious Island Prophecy

JOHN RUSH & ABBE ANDERSON

P.O. BOX 55787   SEATTLE, WA 98155

YWAM Publishing is the publishing ministry of Youth With A Mission. Youth With A Mission (YWAM) is an international missionary organization of Christians from many denominations dedicated to presenting Jesus Christ to this generation. To this end, YWAM has focused its efforts in three main areas: (1) training and equipping believers for their part in fulfilling the Great Commission (Matthew 28:19), (2) personal evangelism, and (3) mercy ministry (medical and relief work).

For a free catalog of books and materials, contact:

YWAM Publishing
P.O. Box 55787, Seattle, WA 98155
(425) 771-1153 or (800) 922-2143
www.ywampublishing.com

The Man with the Bird on His Head

10 09 08 07   10 9 8 7 6 5 4 3

Published by YWAM Publishing
P.O. Box 55787, Seattle, WA 98155

ISBN 1-57658-005-9

Printed in the United States of America.

Other International Adventures

To our family and friends who,
through their vision, prayers and sacrifice,
have changed the world.

Acknowledgments

T H E crafting of this book has been a joint effort not just by two writers but by numerous friends, family and experts without whom this project could not have been completed.

The authors wish to extend their thanks to Sarah Rudd for her research and written contributions to the John Frum background material, Prof. Herbert Ford for his input on the history of Pitcairn Island, Diane Hetfield for her recollections and photos of the John Frum contact, Shari Rush for her help with word processing and Rex and Judy Stevens for the use of their computer and e-mail facilities.

For their encouragement, advice, proofreading and recollections, the writers would like to thank Greg Dryden, Greg Carlson, Bryan Pollard, Ian Crawford, Betty Hanson, Jack and Kay Rudd, Nola and Jim Anderson, Dr. Julia Collett, Jeane Elmlund, Cindy Ryan, Captain Jesse Misa, De and Paul Bretherton, Heather Kendrick, Trudy Rush, Pastor Al Soto, Pastor Rick Benjamin, Pastor Bart Rush, Pastor Chris Haines and Pastor Graeme Lauridsen.

Special thanks goes to Dr. Loren Cunningham, Don Stephens, Dr. Linus Morris and Dr. Art Patzia for their encouragement and support of this project.

The ultimate thanks, of course, goes to the One who wrote this story before creation and has graciously allowed all of us to take part in fulfilling His incredible plan.

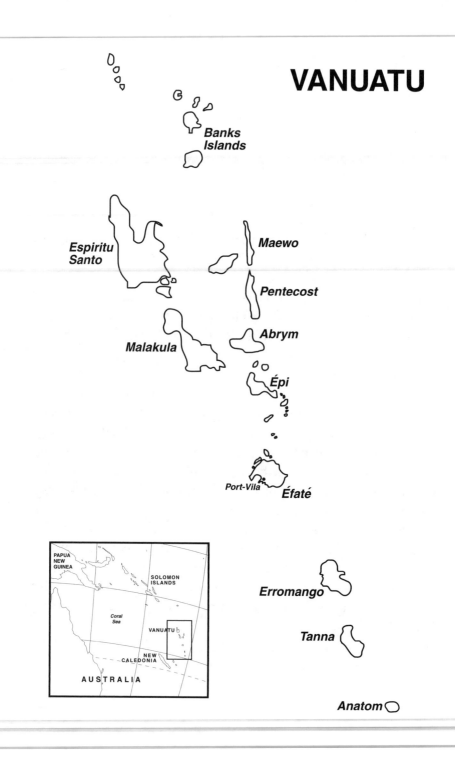

VANUATU

Banks
Islands

Espiritu
Santo

Maewo

Pentecost

Abrym

Malakula

Épi

Port-Vila

Éfaté

PAPUA
NEW
GUINEA

SOLOMON
ISLANDS

Coral
Sea

VANUATU

NEW
CALEDONIA

AUSTRALIA

Erromango

Tanna

Anatom

Contents

Foreword

by Don Richardson

INHABITANTS of Tanna, a little cashew-shaped island in the South Pacific, took a heavy toll on nineteenth-century missionary pioneers. Still, the gospel prevailed until, by the early 1900s, almost everyone on Tanna was at least nominally Christian. Then some elements of the church on Tanna began to "play government." Unlike the early pioneers, they relied less upon the charisma of the Holy Spirit to elicit voluntary self-control on the part of church members. Instead, they legislated and tried to enforce a strict moral code. Some islanders eventually rebelled, forming a cargo cult centered around a heroic being called "John Frum America." Positive contact with World War II American GIs and medics played a major role in providing the "John Frum" movement with its own unique doctrinal base.

In subsequent decades, the John Frum movement firmly resisted efforts by established churches on Tanna to reconcile with them. They chose instead to await the coming of "John Frum America," their Messiah. How could this tragic breach be healed?

Little did John Rush from San Jose, California, realize what awaited him when he stepped ashore on Tanna. John had never planned to play the role of a deliverer, not even as a part in Handel's "Messiah." But deliverer was exactly the role John was called to fill, not on a stage in the Metropolitan but on a real-life plain below Tanna's Mount Yasur, a volcano sacred to the John Frum people. Lessons of compassion, human interest, surprising turns—all await readers who treat themselves to this remarkable true-life adventure.

Don Richardson is the author of best-sellers Peace Child, Lords of the Earth, *and* Eternity in Their Hearts.

Foreword

by Loren Cunningham

I N over forty years of travel across the nations and continents, I have often heard missionaries say, "This is the hardest field on earth. Every door is closed." Others nearby would say with equal conviction, "The door of opportunity is open everywhere. We just don't have enough hours in the day to accomplish all there is to do."

What makes the difference between an open door and a closed door?

The smallest key can unlock a huge door of opportunity. Only the Holy Spirit can give us that key.

The cargo cults of the South Pacific have kept the hearts of the people closed to the gospel with a false hope of material gain. The wickedness of this satanic bondage toward these lovely islanders has been evidenced in the cruelty of this false hope. At least in Western nations where we have materialism we have been able to put our hands on the material things. But the spiritual key is not giving material things; it's feeding the souls of the spiritually starved.

When the YWAM Mercy Ship *Pacific Ruby* arrived in Vanuatu, the islanders had no idea that a young man was aboard who had a key to open the hearts of this isolated community of needy people. John Rush was from America. Therefore, in the people's minds he became John Frum ("From"), the one they were looking for who would somehow answer their needs.

Why was John on that ship? What led him from California and a life of ministry to this remote island? What was it that called him to be the pastor on board the ship at the very time she would pull into this harbor? These "divine coincidences" that I see daily and constantly around the world are a part of the ways of God, who said in His word, "I have put before you an open door which no one can shut, because you have a little power, and have kept My word, and have not denied My name" (Revelation 3:8 NAS).

The story in this book is another encouragement of modern missions miracles. A miracle is simply what God is doing that cannot be explained without Him. Be encouraged, inspired and challenged to be a part of what God is doing throughout the world.

Loren Cunningham is the founder and chairman of Youth With A Mission International.

Prologue

"And the isles shall wait for his law." Isaiah 42:4 (KJV)

*"Our songs are about the love and the law of John Frum
and how we will live forever when John Frum comes."*

L E A V I N G a comfortable salary and position to venture
into a faith-supported ministry is a challenging transition. There have
been times when the magnitude of our career and lifestyle change has
weighed heavily on me.

One sunny New Zealand afternoon, I tossed a Frisbee to my son
Johnny. As he ran along the warm sand to save the rolling disk from
the approaching waves, I noticed with pride how he was growing up.
At the same time, I was struck with a myriad of uncertainties as I suddenly thought, "What will we have for him, Lord? On our little income,
what inheritance will there be for Johnny or for our girls?"

I am certain there are some questions that God has waited a long
time for me to ask just so He can enthusiastically seize the "teaching
moment." With almost overwhelming force, I felt God respond, "You
are your son's inheritance."

I struggled to understand these intriguing words. As I looked
down the broad beach that seemed to stretch from the base of Mt.
Maunganui to forever, I asked the Lord, "What do you mean?"

"If Johnny learns from you how to love Me, his wife and his family, how to keep promises and work hard, how to make friends, laugh
at himself and not let failure dissuade him from pursuing success, how
much money will he need?"

As I pondered this, I answered, "He won't need great wealth, Lord. He will be okay. He will be an honorable, successful and happy man."

To drive the lesson home, God continued, "And if he does not learn these things from you, how much money will be enough to make up for the pain and heartache that he will face?"

I am amazed at how long it can take for us to understand life's realities. God created gold out of nothing. For Him, it is so common that He uses it as paving material in heaven. The Bible makes it clear that our real inheritance has nothing to do with the material trappings of this world but rather has to do with the eternal treasures of relationships.

King David renounced the material riches of life when he said, "The Lord is my inheritance." God, who possesses everything in the universe, has declared, "Israel, my people, are my inheritance." God has chosen *us* as His most precious treasure.

I looked out across the breaking waves to the vast Pacific horizon and recalled the words from the second psalm: "Ask of me, and I will make the nations your inheritance." I thought of the thousands of islands, filled with people, that make up the nations of the South Pacific. In devotion, I asked the Lord, "If it is true that my real inheritance is Your people, give me an inheritance here in the Pacific. Let me reach the hearts of Pacific people as an inheritance that will last forever."

I could never have anticipated the amazing way that God would answer my prayer and use an ordinary man to fulfill an extraordinary purpose.

PART ONE

John Versus the Volcano

ONE

The Man with the Bird on His Head

THE mild humidity and breezy warmth of Vila were a welcome change from a cold and wet New Zealand winter. June must be the perfect time to visit Vanuatu. I unwound from the three-hour flight from Auckland by walking the now familiar streets of downtown Port Vila. The main street here forms a gentle crescent containing a flat, grassy park that runs right up to the seawall and an overlook of Vila Bay. To the left, expensive yachts dot the narrow channel that separates the lovely, teardrop-shaped Iririki resort island from the mainland. In sharp contrast to the poverty of so many in these islands, luxury bungalows line the shores of the bay and draw the eye to the right where, in the distance, the white geodesic dome of Missionary Baptist Church rises on the shore of Ifira island. Farther to the right and opposite Ifira is the Malapoa Peninsula. Together they form the entrance to Port Vila, the cultural and business center of this struggling and newly independent developing Melanesian nation.

As I admired the wooden carvings and other handcrafted items in the shops along the roughly maintained streets, I was arrested by a striking and unfamiliar sculpted image. The smooth and rounded lines of the piece contradicted its comedic portrayal of a man with a bird perched on his head. I had not seen this image before, and I suppose it appealed to me because it portrayed the way I often felt when visiting my newfound island friends on the outlying Vanuatuan island of Tanna. Everyone else seemed to wear a knowing look in my presence that often gave me the impression that there was something peculiar about me. I had become accustomed to those stares on Tanna ever since my first visit there in 1993. Perhaps, like the man in this carving, a bird had come to roost on my head, and this odd passenger was evident to everyone but me.

This wooden man and I have a lot in common, I mused as I considered whether I should buy the piece as a souvenir. Not now, I decided. I would be back through Port Vila in a few days, and if the piece was still in the shop, I would decide then.

Two years earlier, before my bird had come to roost, I was serving as a director on a Christian relief and medical ship called the *Pacific Ruby*. We had just completed three weeks of ministry work in Tonga and Fiji. I was already exhausted from the intense time away from my family, and I was looking forward to my flight home to New Zealand in a little over a week. We were unable to bring the ship alongside the wharf on our first night in Port Vila, a disappointment to many of our crew who were looking forward to an evening ashore after the three-and-a-half-day sail from Fiji in the somewhat confining quarters of our little 140-foot ship.

We were fortunate the next day to be able to up-anchor and come alongside the main wharf situated at the end of the principal road that skirts the perimeter of this beautiful harbor. Our staff and crew were able to take a much needed wander around town. Many took the opportunity to purchase mosquito nets and insect repellents, as we had been aware for some time that the island of Tanna, our next destination, was plagued with a severe form of malaria, a cerebral type that can induce dementia and death. Also at this time we were joined by members of our medical team who had flown into Vila's small international airport to join the ship. Andrew Clark and Steve Morris would be operating medical clinics while optometrist Graeme Butler, who had joined us in Fiji, would be using high-tech equipment to test islanders' vision and dispense hundreds of pairs of donated glasses. Our dental team, Charlie and Nancy Roberts and Ken Anderson, would be joining us once we arrived in Tanna.

That afternoon, as shore leave expired, we sat down to a shipboard dinner as the *Ruby* began her overnight passage to the island of Tanna. The coming week would mark the end of my fourth outreach aboard the *Pacific Ruby*. The lounge where we were eating had become a very familiar place, filled with the faces of people who had bonded together through long hours of crisis, seasickness, work and play. As I looked around the room at this courageous company of friends, I recalled the first time I had met Jesse, a bright and witty, fit Filipino man. I think that the widest part of Jesse is his grin. Quite a contrast to the tall, bulky form that I presented to the company assembled in this same lounge two years earlier when I had joined Mercy Ships for my first voyage. I had flown from Kona, Hawaii, to meet the ship at Rarotonga in the Cook Islands. I was a welcome figure primarily because of the substantial amount of mail I couriered with me.

Jesse, then the first mate, took me below to the small cabin that we would be sharing for the next several weeks. As is typical with many of the ship's forward cabins, there was barely enough space for the two of us to stand together in front of a small desk and wardrobe. Two bunks hung against the sloping port-side bulkhead, each equipped with a frail netting that was hooked to the top to keep you in your bed in the sometimes fifty-degree rolls from amidships to beam. In true Christian deference, Jesse offered me my choice of bunks. I quickly noted that the top bunk seemed longer and that the sloping shape of the hull allowed more room at the top.

"I'll take the top one. It looks roomier."

I could see the look of panic in Jesse's eyes as he looked first at me in my full dimension and then at the top bunk which, if it were a waterfall, would have spilled neatly onto the lower bunk because of the narrower width of the hull at that lower level.

"What's the matter?" I asked.

"You're a big man. If you fall out of your bunk when the ship rolls, you'll kill me and you won't even wake up!"

We both laughed and a long friendship was begun. Tenderfooted seaman that I am, I was going to learn a lot from this consummate merchant mariner. The education on rolling and pitching I would soon learn from the *Ruby* and from the temperamental Pacific itself. There is nothing in the world like living in an environment where the floor is always moving. Up and down, back and forth. I once calculated that in a typical one-week sail, the ship would routinely roll from fifteen to twenty degrees starboard to fifteen or twenty degrees port a total of forty thousand times. At times the ship will roll as much as fifty degrees in one direction which, for the layman, means that for a brief moment it is easier to walk on the walls than the floor. In moments like these, everything that is not nailed down, including people, will fly from one side of a room to the other. Heaven help you if you should be showering at a moment like that. There have been times when I have had to hold the shower head firmly with one hand and try to use the soap with the other, always fearing that my grip would slip and I would be thrown through the shower door, with its flimsy lock, and careen down the smooth, coed hall in a naked soapy blur. "Good to see you, Pastor Rush!"

In those first months, Jesse and I would end up unknowingly prophesying to each other. The first occasion was an evening when we were escorting the ship's nurse and purser to the local island phone service where we would all be making calls to our loved ones. Jesse's wife, Princess, had to return to New Zealand from Rarotonga, as she was in the first trimester of her pregnancy with their firstborn. The combination of mal de mer and morning sickness was enough to drive even this brave woman to retreat onto terra firma. As we walked the occasionally lit streets to Telecom, Jesse said, "John, you haven't just come to be our pastor and team coordinator. Someday you will be this ship's director and I will be the captain—we will work together!"

Now, as we sailed for Tanna, I realized his words had come true. I was serving as the ship's director, and just prior to leaving on this outreach, I had the privilege of seeing Jesse commissioned into his role as captain. At that ceremony in my church, I remember telling Jesse words from John the Baptist: "Jesse, now you must increase in your role as a spiritual leader on the ship, and I will decrease." The words and role of John the Baptist were to become an important hallmark for what the Lord was about to do on Tanna.

Youth With A Mission (YWAM), our parent ministry and the world's largest international Christian service and missions organization, has always cherished directive and passionate prayer as one of its dynamics and distinctives. As we had prepared for our rigorous medical, dental, relief and evangelism outreach to Tanna, the ship's complement had been organized into a number of prayer groups. As these groups focused their attention on the needs of Tanna, they began to report that God had directed them to a number of biblical references to the ministry of John the Baptist. John was the figure who prepared the Jewish public for the emerging ministry of Jesus some two thousand years ago. It appeared from these scriptures that Jesus was going to use us, like John of old, to help many to a life-changing understanding of Christ. When John first introduced the life-giving message of Christ, standing in the Jordan River in ancient Palestine, the message was signaled by a dove that descended from heaven and rested on Jesus.

In the early morning hours of May 1, 1993, we dropped our anchor in the waters near Lenakel village on the island of Tanna. Soon, my own peculiar bird would be making his debut.

TWO

"Is He the One?"

M A N Y peaceful nights aboard ship were interrupted by the intense metallic racket of long lengths of anchor chain being flung out of the chain lockers and plunging into the sea. Some of our crew actually had the misfortune of sleeping in bunks attached to bulkheads of the chain lockers. The noise was outrageous when the heavy eight-inch links would career into the steel walls. As unsettling as this sound was, it was often the welcome sign that the ship had completed its passage and that dawn would reveal yet another challenging destination and the opportunity to go ashore.

The morning sun gave us the light we needed to spy the treacherous reefs that are the real peril when approaching the small and shallow concrete wharf that services the village of Lenakel and the island of Tanna. The wharf had recently been constructed as a gift from the Japanese government, which had funded a number of development projects in Vanuatu since the country's independence from the joint English and French government in 1980.

The wharf is connected to the mainland by a short concrete road that is protected from the onslaught of the sea by a half dozen massive concrete star-shaped retainers. These heavy pylons are about eight feet across and are shaped like jacks from a child's game. The wharf is not well protected from the open sea and is constructed so low that at high tide the waves often sweep completely over it. Bringing the *Ruby* alongside this short, shallow structure proved to be a spine-chilling challenge even for a seasoned navigator like Captain Jesse. The task was further complicated by the limited maneuverability of the *Ruby* with her single rear propeller. To keep the oncoming sea from sweeping us away from the wharf and onto the coral, the ship's inflatable landing craft was deployed to act as a makeshift lateral thruster, pushing against the starboard stern and helping us make contact with the wharf.

The difficulty of this wharf and its approach was often magnified by worsening sea conditions that could stress and snap the large three-inch-diameter lines that secured us to the wharf and prevented the ship from smashing against the concrete dock or the nearby outcroppings of coral. These same dangerous conditions also made it difficult to maneuver the ship in reverse back out to sea, where she could lie at anchor and more safely ride out the swell. The decision whether to stay alongside or to put out to sea was a frequent and tough one for our captain to make and one with enormous consequences. The sea can never be underestimated for its ability to provide no-win situations. The islands of the Pacific are littered with the rusting hulls of gallant maidens whose capable crews faced similar scenarios with unfortunate outcomes. The stress of this continual decision took a clear toll on my friend Jesse.

Upon our initial arrival, the wharf and its short concrete road were covered with Tannese islanders. Young and old had turned out to welcome us. The waters around the ship were filled with a number of hand-lashed, dugout outrigger canoes. The local leaders had long been aware of our planned visit to their villages, and the excitement surrounding our arrival was obvious.

The first few hours were taken up by the activities and preparations for the many facets of our planned work there. A number of cargoes were unloaded, including donated clothing, food, medical equipment and supplies along with a number of personal packages and deliveries.

The medical, optical and dental teams were busy evaluating the small nearby residence that had been made available for their clinic work. Deck crews were arranging for the arrival and intake of fresh water and other necessities by truck. Engineers were attempting to assess the requests for repair of outboard motors, generators and a water tank at the island's nearby hospital.

In addition, leaders of the ship's ministry training school were making contact with island church and school leaders in preparation for their rigorous schedule of evangelism, music, prayer and teaching. Certainly not least, the hospitality staff was busily arranging for the purchase and procurement of local food to keep the ship's thirty-eight workers properly fed.

For my part, in addition to supervising this flurry of activity, I took time to greet and play with the many children on the wharf, to listen to them sing their favorite songs and to meet with island leaders and pastors to plan for the outreach and make arrangements for the island pastors' conference that had been scheduled for the upcoming week. By late afternoon, many of our questions had been asked, and some had even been answered. As the tropic sun began to quickly set, our large island-style welcome was getting under way.

Smelling of mosquito repellent, the *Ruby* team gathered under the large banyan tree near the house that would be our medical clinic. The tree and clinic were situated on the village's main road just across the street from a rugged, crescent-shaped, white-sand beach. The short road to the wharf circled around to the right and out to the *Ruby,* poised against the glowing evening horizon. By day, the area under the banyan tree was the site of an informal open-air fruit and vegetable market, but tonight it had become the entrance of a temporary flowered promenade sloping gently up to a village meeting area.

As a local leader indicated that the preparations were complete, we began our slow approach to the meeting ground. Suddenly, as we reached the entrance, a warrior figure charged from the chief's concrete meeting hall, brandishing a large club and shouting threats. It is a common greeting ceremony in the Pacific, meant to test whether you are friend or foe. Our ministry school leader had been versed on the appropriate response, and we were subsequently welcomed to the party.

Pacific islanders love the art of singing and speechmaking, and they are accomplished at both. A welcome is often marked by a number of heartfelt and well-prepared speeches punctuated by the singing of songs and hymns. Our Western love affair with the transistor has made music a spectator affair, and we have lost the discipline of strong, harmonious community song. I have seen small island children, eyes filled with tears from the fear of singing in public, literally blasting their lungs out with a volume and polish that exceeds any one of us, an example, I feel, of the way in which many of our God-given expressions of art and community have atrophied with the artificial support of modern technology. A friend of my father's once remarked that he remembers bringing home his family's first TV set, because it was on that day that conversation died. I have often felt that I have learned far more from my cherished Pacific friends than I will ever be able to give back to them.

Also lost in Western society is the islander's sense of community, family and history. Islanders' speeches are often marked by a reverential recounting of the life, deeds and agreements of honored patriarchs whose influence is strongly felt. The exchange of speeches this night was highlighted by a Tannese pastor who eloquently stated that his people would be ever grateful to us because it was our European ancestors who had lost their lives to the violence of their forefathers in the process of bringing the precious gospel to them. The people's profound sense of history and community is exceeded only by their overwhelming generosity and willingness to share everything with their guests. It is this entirely non-Western view of shared possession that has been shamefully exploited by missionary, visitor and trader over the centuries. In the past, large portions of the islands' vital male population have been kidnaped to distant South American and Australian plantations on the empty promise of being returned to their island homes and families with great wealth. Some islands lost 50 percent of their men to this slave trade.

To this day, Western businessmen are known to make shady contracts with trusting island chiefs and leaders to secure prime beachfront real estate for exotic resorts and effectively force island people off their own land—land they would have been quite willing to share. My

Tannese friends have frequently offered to provide some property and a thatched home for my family should we decide to live there. Many of these villagers have very little need for money. The land and sea are quite generous to them with a ready supply of food and sheltering materials, while our love of currency and profit has often failed to bring them any real benefit.

The bountifully supplied island welcoming feast of rice and fish, lobster and sweet potato, taro and pork lasted long into the night. Finally, by the light of the moon, we carefully walked our overfed bellies through the tall grass and dark night to the ship. Rolling into our bunks, we were lulled to sleep by the lapping of the swell against the ship.

The next morning, a brightly colored pageant of women and girls in their Mother Hubbard dresses dotted the steep path up to the island's main Presbyterian church. The colorful celebration of dressing up for Sunday church is a feast for the eyes and a prominent feature of Pacific life. The weatherworn yet stately old church is perhaps the oldest structure on the island. One must watch one's step when walking in to avoid falling through some of the more rotten timbers that have become the home to boring insects. Every kind of building material is vulnerable to tropical conditions, and it is quite remarkable that this church is still standing.

The sanctuary was packed, with still more faces peering in through the windows and doors. The singing was deafening in its enthusiasm and strength. On the platform stood only a small table with an embroidered cloth that read simply, "Yumi Praisem God," which properly characterized this people's uncluttered focus on joy and life in Christ. I was told by church elders that I was the first American to preach in this historic place. Our evangelism team also presented some of their music and puppetry with the attentive and gracious congregation.

Following the service was the distinct Tannese custom of hand shaking. We, as their guests, stood in a long line outside the church door as every islander in the service, including children and some babes in arms, was careful to shake every one of our hands on the way out. I think one of our team said he had shaken 380 hands that morning. Following the service, we were treated to another large feast. I took some time to get another look at the sanctuary and to mentally prepare for the weeklong pastors' conference that I would be conducting in this same room starting the next morning.

It is a challenge to teach pastors and leaders anywhere, but it is particularly so when the pastors and leaders are of a vastly different culture with peculiar demands and problems that are simply not the same as those we face in the West. In addition, there is the barrier of language and vocabulary which, combined with the Tannese reluctance to ask or answer questions in a formal church setting, can leave you wondering whether you are getting anything across. Questions that are meant to be interactive often go unanswered. In our opening morning session, as I was presenting my introduction to these thirty to forty leaders, I was unaware that they had something else on their minds. Though I was oblivious to its presence, they could clearly see a bird on my head.

As the session ended, we all moved outside to the shade of some large trees on the brow of the hill where the church overlooked the village, the harbor and our small white ship. As we rested, the leaders began to chat in their local tongues, and one of them approached me. This educated Presbyterian leader spoke good English as he began to tell me about an interesting group of people on their island. I listened with a degree of skepticism as he told me how these people have been waiting for fifty years for a man named John to come from America in a white ship bringing free medical care and other help and cargo. I was amazed to hear how these people had modeled their villages to look like American military bases and how they continue to fly the American flag and march in formation with bamboo replica rifles. The other leaders voiced their agreement as I was told of the church's inability to bring the gospel into these villages. Their efforts were handicapped by the fact that these villagers, known as the John Frum movement, consider themselves to be American citizens and have little use for any help or advice that comes from their fellow islanders.

Finally, I was told that the news of our visit, of a white medical ship with an American director named John, had spread among this group and that the circumstances of our arrival had raised strong expectations among them. The Presbyterian leader, Pastor Willy, explained,

"Pastor Rush, because of the way in which you have come and the things that you are doing, some of them believe that you are 'the one.'"

I found the whole story to be incredible, and I let them know that I was not interested in being anybody's "one" except maybe for my wife and children in New Zealand whom I was very eager to see at the end of the week when I would fly home. While I pondered what sort of strange island politics this was and how I was not interested in getting involved, another Presbyterian leader, Pastor James spoke up. "Pastor Rush, we think that this is the timing of God, a great opportunity for you to go to these people and to their chief and to tell them not to wait for America anymore but to put their trust in Jesus. They will not listen to us, but they will listen to you."

Again, I was clearly disturbed by the idea. Surely this is not my responsibility. I am not a great evangelist or pioneer missionary. What kind of trouble could I get myself and our international ministry into? Not to mention it would interrupt the schedule of our conference. No, I was not interested. I was too tired for this. I wanted to go home. I had done my bit. Perhaps the next American Christian with the uncommon name of John arriving on a white ship could handle this one! Then Pastor Willy said, "Thousands of people here are going to hell because of what the Americans started here during the war. Now what are you, as an American, going to do about it?"

I was stunned by the force of this question, which I was not prepared to answer. I said that I would bring the matter up before the ship's staff that evening and we would pray about the request. We then left our breezy spot under the trees and returned to the church for our next session.

At the end of the day, I walked down the steep hill toward the village. As I passed in front of a small village store, an elderly man walked up to me, leaned on his cane and gazed intently at me. He spoke in his dialect to one of the island pastors with me. They spoke briefly and obviously about me. As the old man walked away, I asked my escort, "What did he want?"

My friend replied, "He is one of the John Frum people. He wants to know if you are the one they have been waiting for."

"What did you tell him?" I asked.

"Well, I tole 'im that you are Pastor John from America and that you have a message from God for them."

"Oh," I replied.

THREE

"I Worship John Frum!"

F O R me, it was one of the highlights of each evening on the mercy ship to meet together in the *Ruby*'s main lounge after dinner to present reports and plan our strategies for the next day. We often engaged in a lot of singing, praying and laughing during these times together. This meeting was no exception, and as I began to discuss the events of my day, the details of the John Frum people and the remarks and requests of the island pastors, the reactions were understandably lighthearted. The session did have the sound of some big practical joke and prompted countless jabs and jests.

"Oh, I'm sorry, I didn't realize you were so important!"

"So you're 'the one,' eh?"

"Please forgive me for standing in front of you, Mr. Frum."

The remarks were often made with a reverential bow. I must admit that before we prayed about the matter, we all had quite a laugh over it.

The request was no laughing matter, however, to the island pastors, who were waiting early the next morning to learn of my decision. I have to be candid in saying that the whole idea was quite unattractive to me and that my own prayers were that the issue would fade away. So I avoided any discussion until the morning break when we again gathered under the trees outside the church. One of the pastors wasted no time in asking, "So what was the decision of your people?"

I tried to diplomatically mumble that we felt it was a cultural can of worms, that I was tired and that the whole thing was just too strange for us to get involved in. It just was not part of our mission statement to fill this kind of shoes. In the middle of my diplomatic speech, one of the pastors interjected, "We have decided what you will do. We have canceled your seminar for this afternoon, and we have arranged for a van to take you to the other side of the island. We will take you to the chief of these people, and you can tell him not to wait for America anymore but to put his trust in Jesus. He will not listen to us, but he will listen to you! You have a chance to lead these people to Jesus."

I am no veteran cross-cultural missionary or fiery evangelist, and quite frankly their confident plan struck terror in me. So I started to pray earnestly that it would rain. If it rains, I thought, there is no way that we will be able to drive into the bush. "O Lord, it does rain a lot here, so let's have a downpour today!" Today was Tuesday. I was to leave by small plane from here on Friday. All we needed was a storm for a couple of days and this strange island fantasy would be over. It wasn't just my fear of these unknown and peculiar people but my very real concern that we could presumptuously perpetuate a belief system that was already quite confused. I did not know whether it was wise to exploit such a set of circumstances even for the best of objectives. As I said, I prayed for rain.

It was a beautiful, sunny afternoon on the island of Tanna as the van arrived to take me with Pastors Willy and James and two or three others over the central mountains to the other side of the island. As apprehensive as I was, I used the hour drive to ask all kinds of questions about the history and beliefs of this chief and his people. On the rough, gravel road to the summit, I asked, "Why is their chief called Isaak One?" I assumed it was because he was expecting to be the first of a whole line of chiefs named Isaak.

"He is called Chief Isaak One because he says a thing only one time," a pastor answered.

The others agreed as they spoke about this chief's reputation as a strong, decisive and capable leader. Isaak was deeply concerned about the quality of life of his people and was devoted to the coming of John Frum. He had systematically and effectively resisted the efforts of the church to influence his people. For some reason, I did not find this information to be encouraging.

As we traversed the summit, a wide panorama of Tanna's eastern coast came into view. To the north lay Tanna's longest and most desolate coast and jungles. Directly ahead was the White Sands area containing a number of villages, and slightly to the south was the volcano.

Yasur volcano is considered to be one of the world's most accessible live volcanos. From a distance you can see why this fearsome, smoking black mountain dominates the lives of those living on this side of the island. At night, its fiery shows can often be seen, like a pyrotechnic display lighting up the dark tropic sky heavy with clouds of steam and ash. As we drove through the small villages on the way to the volcano, we could see the lush green vegetation, corrugated iron roofs and thatched huts all covered with a charcoal-colored dusting of ash. As we drove nearer the volcano, the tropical vegetation gave way to the stark, barren landscape of lava and ash fields surrounding its base. Dark dunes of ash were interrupted by eerie oases of tall, forbidding bushes with spherical clusters of ridged, pointed leaves that resembled an array of small swords—an almost medieval portent of doom.

In the midst of the landscape and at the base of the volcano's steep, ashen slopes was the dark and lifeless reflection of Lake Siwi, deepening the contrast between this region and the lush growth in the distance. My companions told me that the chief and his people's main village was located at the base of this mountain and that, indeed, the mountain was sacred to them, as they regard themselves to be living under John Frum's "giant shadow." My mind wandered back to the silly movie the crew had rented and viewed just a few nights earlier in Port Vila; *Joe Versus the Volcano*—an ordinary Joe, an angry volcano and an island culture with peculiar beliefs. The whole experience began to take on a surrealistic quality.

The van was driven around the lake to the left and then turned to the right to pass between the base of the volcano and the lake. The occasional rumble left no doubt as to the mountain's brooding, untamed power and made me anxious to put some distance between us and this volcanic mass.

In due time, the ash fields again surrendered to the vibrant energy of the tropical bush. One by one, we began to encounter dark-skinned Melanesian men, all with machetes, and some working hard to clear away the growth encroaching on the roadway. The Tannese people are very fit and rugged, and it is not hard for a visitor to be intimidated by their appearance, especially when they are wielding one of their large knives. The van driver would stop from time to time to inquire as to the location of the chief. I was nervous in this remote setting, and just as I was praying that we might not be able to find our man, the van stopped suddenly and the side door was flung open.

"This is Chief Isaak One," someone announced as I looked at the figure standing outside the van door. The chief wore no special attire but was dressed as any of his fellow workers, with loose-fitting slacks and an unbuttoned shirt. He set his knife inside the van and accepted the invitation to join us for a ride to his village. As I sat in the backseat in my uniform and tie and my Mercy Ships name badge, the contrast with his more appropriate dress was marked. I reached out to shake his hand, and my interpreter introduced me. "This is Pastor John Rush from America. He is the director on the hospital ship that is here."

It was clear that he already knew who I was, and he told me that he had been informed about our arrival and work on the island. I began to explain that we were a Christian ministry that was working with the church to help people learn about Jesus Christ.

"I am not interested in the church! I am not interested in Jesus Christ! I worship John Frum!" he said abruptly.

I am not known to be one to give up on most discussions, but with this strong reply, I realized that I had started our relationship on the wrong note, and so I was quite happy to talk about other things. As we made our way to the main John Frum village of Sulphur Bay, I asked the chief a number of questions, little knowing that this drive together would be the beginning of a genuine friendship between two people from vastly different worlds.

I learned that the chief had just been visiting a newly discovered volcano vent to settle a dispute that had arisen about its proper ownership.

The land on Tanna is passed down through families and distributed to the male descendants. The chiefs are responsible for keeping track of the boundaries and landmarks of each person's land. With unexpected deaths, uncertain succession, family feuds and changing vegetation and landscape, this system is far from an exact science. There are no land surveys or corner stakes, just the large tree here to the distinctive rock there, and all is quickly changed by constant and overpowering growth. I am amazed at the amount of information that is passed from an old chief to his successor. In a culture without written language, the memory is very important. I soon gained a great appreciation for this man as I asked about his own family and the needs of his people and as I saw his obvious burden for the improvement of their way of life.

We had picked the chief up on one side of the volcano, and his village was on the other. To get to our destination, we took the van back around the mountain, again skirting Lake Siwi, across the ash fields and down a short road through the bush leading down to the sea. Sulphur Bay is the name of the community and the gently curved white-sand-rimmed bay on which it sits. From the beach, you can see the smartly fenced village with the dark ash cone and belching smoke rising from the volcano above it. Every now and then, the ground trembles with the thunder of another eruption. Brave souls live here.

When we arrived at Sulphur Bay, I was immediately struck with the features of this well-kept community. The road ended at the main entrance to the village. The entry was simply a portion of the stockade-style wooden fence that was reduced to a height that an adult could straddle. The rest of the fence was about five feet high and extended around the main area, with straight lines and right-angled corners that were more reminiscent of a military base than a casual Pacific settlement. The obvious military imitation was clearly reflected in the immaculate thatched homes that lay in straight lines around a central parade ground and meeting area. In the distance was a lone flagpole flying the flag of the U.S. Marine Corps, while near us at the entrance were four flagpoles. One flew the flag of Vanuatu's southern district of islands; another, the flag of the U.S. Navy; the next, America's Stars and Stripes. I noticed the last pole was bare and quickly wondered whether I would be strung up on it by the end of the day.

It was quite strange to see the flag of my home country flying over this Melanesian community, but as the chief showed me the John Frum church, the John Frum headquarters and other American and military artifacts, I realized the strong devotion of these people to an ideal and mythology that was clearly beyond my ability to comprehend. I openly expressed to the chief my admiration for his village, its fine construction and clear design. As our visit came to an end, the chief unexpectedly extended a gracious invitation to bring a group of our workers to his village on Thursday to present our message to his people. I was quite heartened at his openness, and the interpreters and pastors with me soon hammered out the details of the group's arrival in just two days. I cautioned them that our visit would be contingent on the advice of the other leaders on the ship, as I was still unsure about the wisdom of any further involvement.

On the way back across the island, the others in the van reassured me that our visit had been very successful, as it was remarkable to have such an open invitation from Chief Isaak One. They talked about the impact I had as an American on this stalwart chief. I remember feeling as I had felt from the beginning of this affair—that the whole thing was happening in spite of me. Was I being carried along by the force of God's loving appointment to fulfill these people's long years of expectation, or was it just a rather comedic set of circumstances? I struggled to grasp the situation. Who was I to these special people?

FOUR

"America Is Coming to Tanna"

B Y most accounts, the Western world was first introduced to Tanna in 1774 with the arrival of Captain James Cook. Captain Cook is credited with being the first European to explore and chart countless islands and coastlines across the vast Pacific. He "discovered" Tanna by following the red glow he observed on the horizon late one night—the fiery glow of Yasur. He sailed into a sheltered inlet near the base of the brooding volcano, naming the area Port Resolution after his ship, HMS *Resolution*. In his two-week stay, Cook befriended an elderly chief named Paowang. Trying to ascertain the name of the island, Cook pointed to the ground. Possibly thinking Cook wanted to know the word for "ground," Paowang helpfully replied "muk-tana," which is how Tanna was named.

Just days before arriving in Tanna, Cook, in need of firewood and fresh water, had attempted to land at Erromango island, just north of Tanna. Cook became alarmed as his shore party was met by a multitude of armed islanders who surrounded his launch and tried to haul it ashore. He ordered his men to shoot, killing four Erromangans. He later wrote, "It is impossible for them to know our real design. We enter their Ports and attempt to land in a peaceable manner. If it succeeds all is well, if not we land nevertheless and maintain our footing by the Superiority of our firearms. In what other light can they first look upon us but as invaders of their Country?"[1]

Now that Cook had placed Tanna on the map, more strangers began to arrive, bringing mysterious possessions and news of a world beyond Tanna's shores. To the Tannese, what the white men had and could do was nothing short of magical. To the white man, what the Tannese had was of great value. Sandalwood, for instance, was highly prized but no longer available in Asia. Here it was plentiful. Traders came, soon depleting the abundant supply and leaving the Tannese bereft of this natural resource. Before long, other, more devious men arrived to rob the islands of a much more precious resource—their men. Slave ships came, promising to take Tannese men to other parts of the world and return them in three months with the wealth and magic of the West. As this practice of "blackbirding" continued, islanders began to refuse to go on these trips, knowing the others had never come back. So ships' captains employed new tactics, luring the island men aboard their ships to see cargo they had brought for trade or even inviting them to attend supposed church services on board. Those trusting men were often never seen again by their families and friends. Thus began Tanna's volatile relationship with the Western world.

The following centuries brought an onslaught of devoted, goodhearted missionaries to the thousands of Pacific islands. One hearty soul, a British man by the name of John Williams, is still revered for his work in the South Pacific. Employing the use of ships, Williams reached many islands with the life-changing message of Jesus Christ. Their trust restored through Williams's selfless dedication, many native converts eagerly sailed with John to other islands to spread the gospel. Unlike the blackbirders before him, Williams kept his word and returned his friends safely to their island homes. But not everyone knew that he could be trusted. In 1839, John Williams's ship arrived in a small bay on the western coast of Erromango island. Visible from Tanna's northern coast, Erromango is Tanna's nearest neighbor. No doubt eager to set foot on solid ground after a long sail and to share his message of peace and love, Williams unknowingly disembarked his ship for the last time. He was met ashore by a cannibalistic tribe who didn't take time to discover whether this white man was friend or foe. Determined that Williams's death would not be in vain, the crew sailed on to Tanna where, although it was too dangerous for the Europeans to stay, a number of the Samoan crew members remained. The Samoans established and maintained a Christian work for nineteen years before the first European missionaries were able to return and settle in Tanna.

Undaunted by such sacrifices, other early missionaries remained devoted to bringing the gospel of Jesus Christ to the islands. But along with the good news, many brought harsh systems of rules and unwavering condemnation of traditional island practices, or "kastom." Some would not rest until they had "civilized" the islands, replacing island traditions and kastom with European traditions and customs. In Tanna, people were forced to comply with the "Tanna laws," which prohibited traditional clothing and forbade customary rituals, dances and feasting to celebrate events such as birth, the naming of children, a boy's circumcision, a girl's first menses, marriage and death. Included in the law was a ban on drinking kava—a beverage made from crushed kava roots that produces a somewhat sedative effect. Kava drinking represented a central part of island ceremonies all over the South Pacific. In Tanna, kastom was halted. The church ran every aspect of life in a crushingly legalistic fashion.

Later, along with the strict rule of the church came the formation of a new Western government. Geographically part of the New Hebrides chain, Tanna fell under the Anglo-French condominium government—an arrangement of joint rule by both Britain and France. To this day, children go to either a French- or an English-speaking school. The most popular speech, though, seems to be a unique variation of pidgin English called Bislama. And so, as the twentieth century marched onward in a land where time is virtually meaningless, the Tannese found themselves seeking a new identity as their old ways were slowly declining under the influence of Western civilization.

Before I went with the *Pacific Ruby* to Tanna, had I known of the existence of this strange segment of Tanna's culture and had I spent time in research, I would have discovered the numerous, curious tales of the origin of the John Frum movement. It seems, in fact, that the John Frum people are one of the South Pacific's best-known cargo cults, having been documented in books and on television and even featured in *National Geographic*. But as it was, even with my longtime fascination with the history and mystique of the South Pacific islands, I, like most Americans, had never even heard of a cargo cult. And yet, regardless of my ignorance, it is a fact that the South Pacific is littered with countless numbers of tribes and peoples who have developed religious belief systems influenced by and formed around the bewildering "magic" of the West. And of the hundreds of so-called cargo cults, no two are exactly alike. Each island, each people over the years, has shaped its own religion according to its particular experiences and circumstances. These belief systems are intricate and changeable and not fully understood by anyone.

On Tanna, stories of the origin of John Frum are equally complex and numerous. It is popularly believed that the first John from America arrived circa 1930. The earliest written records about John Frum date to 1940 and were recorded by a British colonial district agent, a Presbyterian missionary and a local official. Perhaps a Christian missionary who opposed the oppressive and legalistic teachings of the established church, John Frum (the pidgin spelling of "from") upheld and defended the dignity of the traditional Tannese way of life. Missionaries had told the Tannese that the Europeans' wealth was due to regular prayer and renouncing of kastom, but the Tannese had discovered that even if they followed this advice, they did not appear to prosper. The Europeans still seemed to have everything, while the Tannese had only their pigs and gardens. The people, frustrated with the Tanna laws, saw John Frum as a savior and readily returned to their own kastom.

Sam Tacuma, a Tannese man, exemplified the feelings toward John Frum. "John came to lead us out of bondage. When the missionaries came they stopped our Custom....We wonder why the missionaries stopped us. Then John came to lead us from the bondage of the mission."[2] Thus, John Frum became the liberator who had come to take the Tannese people back to their old customs and give them a new life. After he left, narratives about him spread, and more power was attributed to those who knew him. According to some, John Frum would eventually return from America bringing a better religion. An entire belief system evolved with John Frum as the central figure. Integrating teaching from the church about Jesus, the Tannese created their own Messiah who had granted them liberty to retain their own identity and who would return bringing joy and prosperity and, most of all, eternal life. The John Frum following became so strong that the church doors on Tanna were nailed shut and the church leaders expelled.

A television documentary, *Pacifica*, featured the John Frum people saying, "John Frum is both black and white. He is both American and Tannese. He has been seen and equally not seen….He is with us. He is the reincarnation of our ancient god. Through him our past magic lives on."[3] Mellis, a man from Tanna, explains his belief. "Who is John…I will explain once more. Kalbapen represents the European word for God. In other words, John is the son of Kalbapen….I myself think that John is Kalbapen. John is God."[4] Sam Tacuma tells us this story. "When the earth was formed the first man was Kalbapen. When John came, he said he was the Son of Kalbapen….John must be someone sent by God, because…John came here…and when he brought back kastom, I thought it must be someone God knows."[5]

In the Yimwayim, a clearing and gathering place underneath the immense banyan trees, the Tannese gather for their festivals, meetings and storytelling. The Tannese have a chosen few who are appointed to hear from John Frum, like ancient prophets. One such man, Man-Tanna, explains, "No one has written down what John has said. We keep it in our minds."[6] Because it is an oral tradition, it is difficult to trace the exact history of John Frum. Under the banyan trees, the stories and myths evolved with each telling and retelling. Some believed that John Frum was still with them, living in their ancient and forbidding volcano. Others said that John was the volcano and that they lived under the giant shadow of John Frum himself. But the legends surrounding the figure known as John Frum America had only just begun.

In 1942, World War II reached Tanna's shores. Before long, the quiet Pacific islands were involved in a battle they knew nothing about. The Allies took up position on strategic islands. American soldiers built bases, camps, wharves and airstrips, and soon hundreds more arrived by boat and aircraft. The islanders observed everything, dumbfounded by this new wave of Western "magic." Even more incredible, some of the soldiers were black like them, and they too possessed and shared in the magic! This fact confirmed to the John Frum faithful that America held the key to their salvation, that America must be heaven and that America had come to Tanna to save them!

Further accounts of the John Frum history hold that an American military man named John freely distributed medical supplies and care to the Tannese islanders. The Tannese noticed his red cross symbol, so similar to the cross the missionaries revered and worshiped. They noted too that wherever there was a red cross, there was free medical help. Soldiers also freely shared other items from clothing, helmets and flak jackets to food, knives and cigarettes. The islanders marveled at the machinery and equipment—the guns that the soldiers carried so carefully as they marched precisely in straight lines wearing their matching uniforms. The soldiers didn't farm or raise animals, yet their supplies continually arrived. They lived in different-looking villages; their Yimwayim was a central parade ground not under a banyan tree but under tall, skinny poles with colorful flags waving at the top, representing the marvelous land from which they had come. To the Tannese, the military routines and exercises certainly appeared to be some new sort of religious devotion.

Then one day, as suddenly as they had arrived, the Americans were gone. The war had ended, and a cargo cult had begun. Similarly, all over the Pacific, confused island natives waited for the soldiers to return. In some places, islanders diligently and hopefully cleared new airstrips out of dense vegetation, expecting their efforts to bring the planes just as they had observed before. When none arrived, they built wooden replica airplanes and parked them on their carefully maintained runways in hopes of drawing the silver birds back. Still none came. Other islanders built makeshift docks out into the sea to attract ships. When no boats arrived, they could not understand what they had done wrong.

On Tanna, the John Frum people built themselves new villages to replicate the military compounds. They built long rows of huts with sharp, square corners like the American buildings, situated around a central parade ground complete with tall, slender bamboo poles flying the precious flags the Americans had left behind. Around the perimeter of their new village, they built a tall stockade-style fence. Near the parade grounds they built two larger buildings—a John Frum headquarters to house all the sacred artifacts the soldiers had given them and a John Frum church with a bright red wooden cross at the front. And for one last flagpole, they made themselves a new flag, a red cross on a white field, the new symbol of the John Frum movement.

With religious zeal, they faithfully constructed and maintained their village, and yet no one returned. They had built their new home close to the sea with an empty dock jutting out into a peaceful harbor. The book *John Frum He Come* tells of the construction of a dock and large warehouse "constructed for the Cargo from the great white ship that even now is on its way."[7] But no boats arrived, no planes landed. The Americans were not drawn back. Despite the abandonment, the movement grew, and many more John Frum villages were constructed around the island. Soon red crosses were erected all over the island, a display of the people's undying faith and hope in John Frum. Some said that John had thousands of troops waiting in the volcano and that when he returned he would call them forth. A regular pilgrimage was started, carrying a large wooden cross from their low seaside village to the rim of Yasur. If the volcano rumbled, it meant that John had seen them and spoken his approval.

Over time, more pilgrimages developed. On the fifteenth of February, amidst lavish preparations and much excitement, hundreds of pilgrims would travel with their families from all over the island to gather around a red cross in the center of the village. "The pilgrims make their way home in little groups, expecting to meet their messiah at each bend in the road."[8] But still, John did not return. So a people with little concept of time resolved to wait. In the meantime, they would do all they could to remain faithful to John Frum America. They publicly declared themselves to be Americans, proudly flying the Stars and Stripes over their villages. They refused to participate in Tannese society, to work or send their children to schools. The other island residents who no longer believed in Frum's return mocked the John Frum people and angrily accused them of being lazy, for indeed it seemed all they did was wait patiently for the return of John Frum. In defense, the John Frum people boldly proclaimed that they need not work, for when John Frum returned he would bring great wealth and possessions and everything they could ever need or want. They need not educate their children, for when John Frum returned he would build a school and teach everyone everything he needed to know in fifteen days! John Frum would return, and he would greatly reward those who had waited faithfully.

But just how long would they have to wait?

FIVE

Praying for Rain

T W O days! As the van delivered me safely back to the ship, my mind raced over all the arrangements that would have to be made so quickly if we were going to take teams to the John Frum village in just two days. That is, if we decided it would be a wise thing to do. That evening, the ship's complement assembled for the nightly community meeting. There was a tangible atmosphere of amazed excitement as I began to describe the outcome of the day's meeting with the chief. One by one, students and staff began to relate the results of their own prayers regarding the situation. Some had conducted impromptu research to learn more about the John Frum people. We were astounded by articles some had discovered in travel guides, such as *The Lonely Planet*, confirming the existence and describing the beliefs of the John Frum people. The articles spoke of the belief that John Frum America would one day return, perhaps on a ship, bringing free medical help and the answers to all of life's concerns. It was becoming evident that we were in the midst of a staggering and unexpected divine appointment.

As the meeting progressed, the discussion continued. By some accounts, it had been exactly fifty years since the first John Frum appearances, while other sources indicated it had been even longer. Our visit, it seemed, happened to fall at the same time of the year as these somewhat mythical historical appearances. As more of the story of the complicated history of the John Frum people unfolded, our incredulity grew. Never in my wildest dreams could I have imagined something like this. It was pointed out that John Frum had been linked by one of their prophets to the person of John the Baptist. Our recollection was stirred of the clear references to John the Baptist's mission and message that had dominated our prayerful preparations for this outreach.

I remained reluctant and cautious about the whole matter. Though I was excited about the invitation to take an evangelism team into their village, I was still very uneasy about the mythical overtones and possible negative impact of our presence there—especially *my* presence. Would agreeing to lead a team to Sulphur Bay, the heart of the John Frum villages, indicate that I was prepared to see myself, even reluctantly, as the fulfillment of this people's expectations? A willingness to do so seemed laden with presumption. But if this was a divine appointment, as the Tannese pastors had concluded, it would be wrong for me to ignore it. Perhaps this *was* God's timing for this people. Perhaps He had been preparing them and their leader for such a time as this. The invitation from Chief Isaak One was miraculous in the eyes of the island pastors. I had been told that Isaak truly was a wise and caring leader of his people, concerned for their well-being more than his own power or authority. Isaak had been the first chief to allow his children to attend schools, and he had even involved himself in national politics. In 1980, Tanna and the other New Hebrides islands achieved independence from England and France, renaming their islands Vanuatu. Chief Isaak One had traveled to Europe as part of the delegation seeking independence. He was clearly a progressive leader, and perhaps this was all part of God's design. But it just seemed so… unbelievable!

Weariness was overtaking me, and I hoped a good night's sleep in my little bunk would refresh my perspective. I eventually fell asleep to the sounds of the hull scraping against the concrete wharf, the lines straining ominously as the swell intensified. I awoke very early and began to prepare for the day. The predawn motion of the ship corresponded with my thoughts on the John Frum situation—an out-of-control roller-coaster ride. As I prayed I was reminded that God would remain in complete control.

I noted that the ship seemed to be moving more than usual while tied up alongside a dock. In the captain's cabin, Jesse was arising and opening his shutters to observe the day's weather. He too was concerned by the excessive movement of the ship. At that moment, one of the vital mooring lines lashing the ship to the dock snapped under the stress. Overnight, several of our lines had severed, leaving only one bow line and two stern lines, which were now under multiplied stress and threatened to snap at any moment. I felt the uncharacteristic lurch of the vessel as she now moved even freer than before. I knew we were dangerously close to coral outcroppings that could readily shred the steel hull of the *Ruby*.

By the time I reached the bridge of the ship to see what was happening, the deck and engineering crew were already springing into action. Awakened by the snapping line and surging vessel, the crew members were manning their stations. In his shorts and t-shirt, Jesse was yelling out orders to linesmen on the dock and bow of the ship. The bells to the engine room were ringing, and I was requested to man the engine room telegraph, relaying the captain's orders to the engineers below. The helmsman anxiously awaited the captain's orders, taking note of the waves breaking only meters away on jagged, black rocks and reef. The only way to evacuate the wharf was in reverse, straight back for some distance and then swinging to the left to avoid another dangerously shallow area. The swell was pounding the ship from the starboard side and pushing the ship sideways into the wharf. The problem for Captain Jesse was to time our escape just right, between swells. If he missed it by even a few seconds, the waves could push the ship sideways into the reef once we were clear of the dock. The danger was greatly increased by the fact that on the *Ruby* there is a several-second delay between the time the captain gives the order and when the engines actually take effect.

There was no time to waste, as our remaining lines could not hold the ship for long. Everyone was now in place, and the large diesel electric motors had been brought to life. Captain Jesse was riveted to his task. I watched with admiration as my very personable Filipino friend with his sharp wit and strong sense of humor became so concentrated on his job. At times like this, it appeared that nothing could distract him. Jesse not only was assessing all that was being accomplished around him but also was urgently sending up prayers to God to guide and guard the defenseless ship. If there is one thing true of Jesse it is that he is a man of prayer in every circumstance, always relying first and foremost on his Lord.

Jesse gave the order to release all but one of the lines. He would attempt to use the last line as a pivot point for greater control of the ship. He called out instructions for the helm and ordered the engines slow astern. Stepping out to the bridge wing for a better view, he mentally calculated the intervals between swells. The engines were finally beginning to move the ship. Jesse called for half astern and ordered the final line to be released. The ship shuddered and vibrated as the engines gradually increased power. Captain Jesse's eyes were fixed on the rocks so close off our port side. Jesse called for full astern. "Quickly, John!" The ship was nearly clear of the dock, but she wasn't moving fast enough. The next swell was approaching. There was nothing anyone could do now; we were at the mercy of the sea. We were being pushed perilously close to the coral reef. The color was draining from Jesse's brown face as he watched helplessly. It seemed like an eternity, and no doubt our prayers were rapidly accumulating in heaven. At what seemed like the last possible moment, the engines finally took hold and the ship shot backward into the open waters. Jesse quickly called for the engines to be slowed and the helm to be altered to avoid the shallow areas behind us. He consulted the charts and chose an appropriate anchorage and called for the engines to stop and the anchor to be dropped. It had been only minutes since our rude awakening, but the tense morning moments made it feel like we had already had a long day!

We were now faced with the logistical problems of transporting people back and forth from ship to shore and vice versa. The landing craft had already been deployed and brought our linesmen back aboard, and a schedule was worked out for other essential trips. The heavy swells and strong winds made it equally dangerous for the small rubber inflatable to be maneuvering near the reefs and concrete dock. We also faced the problem that the *Ruby's* freshwater tanks were low. We had expected a delivery of fresh water by truck the day before, but it had not arrived. That meant we would have to go back alongside at least one more time when the water truck did show up. Captain Jesse insisted we would do so only when the winds and swells had died down.

When everyone had recovered from the morning's adventure and had had a chance to shower, dress and have breakfast, our daily meeting of the ship's leadership team commenced. After briefly discussing the freshwater and transport situations, the conversation quickly turned to John Frum. The rest of the meeting was consumed with the questions that this opportunity raised. There were discussions about who would be free to make the trip the following day and how the ministry schedules could be rearranged to accommodate the fullest possible presentation. It was decided that the medical clinics would continue in their present location on this side of the island, but virtually all of the evangelism teams would be rescheduled to visit the John Frum village.

The principal discussion, however, had to do with the cultural issues that preoccupied me. We were all excited about the opportunity to present God's message of love to these special people, but would our visit only serve to further confuse and perpetuate a belief system that was already quite extraordinary? I asked for sincere counsel on whether I should go or remain behind. Everyone seemed to feel that it was important for me to go, in that I was their invited guest. Jesse stated that he felt that I had been the most cautious person there as it related to these developments and he felt that I would continue to exercise proper discretion. I said I would ask the island pastors their opinion that morning and would submit to their decision.

My remaining apprehensions were answered when Graeme, our training school leader said, "These people have already been confused by the influence of our culture. If this is a God-given opportunity to present the gospel of Jesus Christ, the benefits far outweigh the risks."

The logic of his statement was a final confirmation of our need to go. We realized that the moment must be seized. With all its curious complications, we had the opportunity to share the life and hope of Jesus Christ with our brothers and sisters in the John Frum movement. I must admit, I still hoped that God would veto the whole plan with a well-timed rainstorm!

At the pastors' conference that day, I carefully asked my Tannese colleagues whether they felt I should accompany the evangelism team the next day. I expressed that much had been accomplished already and perhaps it was an unnecessary complication for me to go back. The pastors were all agreed that it was vital for me, as an American spiritual leader, to return and take the opportunity to encourage the people away from their passive dependency on the American expectation and toward an active faith in Jesus Christ, that is, if the weather improved. At this time, it looked as if my prayers would be answered and our next day's visit might be impossible.

Rain blew and swirled about the open windows and doors of the old Presbyterian church as I continued my presentation to the pastors. We discussed the importance of Bible study as well as the stresses on the personal life of a pastor and his family. The pastors asked about how they could learn to work together even though they had differences in their beliefs and practices. It was clear that God was using this first of its kind combined conference to focus the island pastors more on their shared similarities than on their differences. They were seeing a vivid example of the fruits of working together to reach out to their own island people.

Pacific churches are often plagued with ideological alienation, and the fact that pastors were coming together for this conference was a powerful statement to island residents. On Tanna, like other Pacific islands, pastors are held in high regard as island and village leaders. The fact that these pastors had come together to be taught by an American pastor named John was certain to have an effect on the John Frum community as well.

The John Frum mystique is a part of the experience of every Tannese family. As we concluded the conference, one of the Presbyterian elders took me aside to show me where the doors of the old church had once been nailed shut by his own grandfather. Decades ago, when the John Frum movement had dominated the entire island, virtually everyone's grandparent had become a follower. The churches were abandoned, and the schools on the island, which were operated by the church, were closed. After all, when John Frum returned, he would teach everyone all they needed to know in fifteen days!

In the afternoon, I cautiously descended the muddy slopes of the hill to the village of Lenakel and to the wharf. A number of the crew had come from their work in evangelism, medical clinics and construction and were gathered, waiting to board the inflatable launch that would take us over the surf and swell to where the *Ruby* lay safely anchored.

The stormy weather amplified my melancholy mood that Wednesday night, as it would be perhaps my last onboard community meeting. The following night would be a working night out for our school teams, and therefore no formal meeting would be held on board. I was scheduled to fly home on Friday to New Zealand, where my family's application for residency was being reviewed. If our application was not approved, service on the next outreach would be difficult if not impossible, and our future would be uncertain. But one thing remained sure: My love for these wonderful ministry partners was going to make this farewell difficult.

After our regular time of singing and announcements, our meeting took on a somber tone as I spoke from Philippians about Paul's love for his coworkers and how I was finding myself with the same feelings for so many of them. We then began to pray for the John Frum people. As the momentum of prayer started to build, God began to touch our hearts with a profound sense of love and burden for these special people. One by one, we began to cry out to the Lord to bless the people with a living relationship with Jesus Christ. We began to realize the significance of the scriptures that had surfaced about the role of John the Baptist in pointing the way to Christ. Just as they had so eloquently apologized for the violent deeds of their ancestors toward the early missionaries, we began to confess and repent, in prayer, that our war effort in the Pacific had left behind not a life-giving testimony of Jesus Christ but a twisted and empty hope in a Western millennial dream.

My own heart was changing from fear and apprehension over the consequences to an overriding compassion for my friend Isaak One and his people. I ended the meeting that night with a heartfelt request that if the weather prevented me from going the following day, the team would make the time to go sometime before the ship's departure in a few days. The team members assured me that they would follow through even if I was unable.

I went up to the bridge of the ship to be alone with my thoughts and end my day in prayer. At night on the bridge, all lights are extinguished to provide for a better view outside, creating a feeling of solitude like none other. With no lights to be seen on shore, the only way to remain oriented is through the use of radar. I relieved the officer on anchor watch and agreed to keep an eye on the green glowing radar screen to make sure the anchor kept us firmly in position.

I watched the rain as it pressed in from all sides, spattering against the many windows surrounding me on the bridge. The previously welcome weather had now become a prison, an obstacle to my own desire to see my John Frum friends. In the silence, I began to discuss my thoughts with God and prayed earnestly for the weather to clear. Prayer, real prayer, really does change things—usually by changing us.

"I Know This Is a Holy Book"

T H E R E is perhaps nothing more beautiful than a crystal-clear sunrise over the sparkling Pacific Ocean. I have seen islands where the water is so clear you can gaze over the side of the ship and see the anchor chain played out below the vessel and the anchor lying solidly on the bottom of the ocean many meters below. Amazing schools of fish, sharks and whales are frequently spotted swimming to their undersea destinations or investigating the vibrant turquoise reefs. I emerged from my dark, porthole-less cabin to view the dazzling scene of a cloudless blue sky blending on the horizon with the deep indigo of the sea. Off the port side of the ship lay the pristine island of Tanna, washed clean by the rain of the previous day. Its white beaches and green trees waited silently for a new day to begin.

The seas had calmed, and I found Jesse preparing to take the *Ruby* back alongside the precarious Lenakel wharf. Our precious fresh water was waiting on the dock in a small tanker truck that had finally arrived—only two days late! After breakfast, the department managers and I worked out the logistics for the ministry team's trip to Sulphur Bay. The bulk of the available space in the two vans was taken up by the training school students who were prepared with a variety of presentations. I was left with only a few seats open for the people I wished to bring along. I did my best to select the right people of the many capable and willing crew.

I asked Jesse whether Gary Peters could be released from his duty as the ship's second mate so that he might join me. Gary was a retired officer of the U.S. Navy Submarine Corps. In the providence of God, Gary and his wife Rosella had joined the *Ruby's* outreach but were able to serve only during this two-week time in Tanna. I realized that it was probably no coincidence that Gary was with us for this special appointment, and I felt that his presence, in his Mercy Ships uniform, was important.

Also on the team were Diane Hetfield, a photographer, and Teri-Lynn Haddox, one of the school leaders who had shown an extreme sensitivity to the Holy Spirit's guidance in the John Frum contact. I had asked Teri-Lynn to come along, keep praying and let me know whatever God might speak to her. Finally, in addition to our cook Ron, our purser Jenni and her hardworking husband Craig, released from his duties as fourth officer, we were joined by Pastor Willy and by Harry, our Scripture Union interpreter and guide.

We gathered near the medical clinic at 11 A.M. to board the vans. I took a moment to pray for the trip and to outline our goals to the team. Our first priority would be to lift up Jesus, not America or the West, as the answer to this people's longings for a better life. Secondly, we were hoping that our visit and message would result in an invitation from the chief for further contact and opportunities to share the love of Christ—simply, that the people would want more of what we had to offer. I said that I would like the team to give its presentation and then I would ask whether Gary, Pastor Willy, Harry and I could meet with the chiefs to discuss future involvement.

The doors to the vans were rolled shut, and we began the slow climb over Tanna's central summit. Once again we passed through the lush tropical bush and onto the dark volcanic landscape that surrounds Yasur volcano. The volcano was actively venting enormous clouds of gas and steam. Puffs of ash seemed to punctuate the mountain's many somber moods.

The fiery mountain, with its dark and barren volcanic plain, stood like a sentinel between us and our destination, looming above and beside the main John Frum village. Many times a day, the thunderous tremors and heavenly displays remind villagers that this is John Frum's domain and his sacred mountain. As we neared the volcano, I too was reminded of this powerful presence. Yasur rumbled, shaking the ground and spewing another cloud of ash and steam into the air. It is no wonder that our medical teams encountered so many people with asthma on this side of the island.

Our fragile vans, dwarfed by the immense mountain, crept across the black, ashen plain carrying a new message of hope to these unique people. I had been told that a prominent John Frum prophetess, Elizabeth, who is credited with interpreting the fiery voice of Yasur, had once said that John Frum and John the Baptist were one and the same. As Yasur rumbled yet again I imagined John's voice proclaiming the new message, "Prepare ye the way of the Lord! Behold the Lamb of God! Every valley will be raised up and every mountain brought low."

Skirting the base of the volcano, we circled around to the narrow valley road that opened up to reveal the main John Frum village, with the beach of Sulphur Bay extending to the rocky coast on either side. In the two days since my previous visit, the villagers had worked hard to prepare a wonderful welcome for our team. We were quite surprised to see that our hosts had constructed a stone-lined walkway with flowered arches leading to an entry in the village's wooden fence. As we left our vans and formed a long line in front of the garlanded archway, a score of colorfully dressed women came out to greet us and presented us with fragrant floral leis. I was then presented with a second lei, and we were asked to follow the women through the arches and into the village.

As we entered the village, we were met by a large group of islanders, some dressed in old military jackets and helmets. Some were playing guitars or pounding on drums made from old military supplies, and all were singing in the beautiful and powerful harmonies of the Pacific. My interpreter said, "This is the John Frum band. They are singing the John Frum hymns."

As we walked slowly across the parade grounds toward the meeting area on the other side, I asked, "What are the songs about? What are they singing?"

Pastor Willy spoke up, "They are singing 'America is coming to Tanna. America is coming to save us. America is coming to Tanna to help us.'"

We passed the unusual sight of the U.S. Marine Corps flag flying above us on the left and could see the American and U.S. Navy flags flying in the distance on our right. As a new song began, Willy said, "This song is about your flag. They are singing 'America, for years we have flown your flag. We have suffered because we fly your flag, but still we fly your flag, and we are waiting for America to come.'"

I was overwhelmed by the strangeness and power of this people's beliefs, symbols and expectations. Was this the visitation that they had long awaited? What was for us a very surreal set of circumstances was for them the possible fulfillment of over fifty years of faithful waiting. My knees felt suddenly weak. My mind raced with a dozen questions and insecurities. I slowly shook my head and wondered what all this meant.

One by one, we greeted and shook hands with the chiefs from the other approximately twenty-five John Frum villages on the island. Although this was the main John Frum village, it was by no means the largest. Of the 5,000 to 7,000 people who are a part of the movement, only about 250 live in the main village. From the size of the crowd, it seemed probable that people from some of the neighboring John Frum villages also were in attendance.

Isaak One, the head chief, gave an opening speech and requested a young girl from the village to read to the crowd a letter he had composed. The girl had translated the message into English and timidly stood to read it before the entire crowd before giving the written copy of the letter to me.

I have great and all respect to give a warm welcome to all here in John Frum Head Quarter. We are happy to meet you as a friends of John Frum. I would like to tell you that we have been putting up your flag since 1957. We face many problem about your flag but we still keeping it until today. So today we are really happy to meet you and to tell you that we have prepared your place to stay here and help us. So we want bigger hospital and good education. Better Stop here. Hope to hear from you very soon. Chief

As the letter was handed to me, our team was invited to present what we had prepared. I extended the greetings of our company and led the ship's crew in a couple of our favorite songs while the training school students prepared for their presentation. As we had done many times, the crew sang out, "Glory, glory Lord, we give You glory Lord / You who go down to the sea, you who live in the islands, lift your voice and sing / glory, glory Lord."[1] Then, presenting the gospel message in these simple lyrics, we sang, "You came from heaven to earth, to show the way / from the earth to the cross, our debt to pay / from the cross to the grave, from the grave to the sky / Lord, I lift Your name on high!"[2]

By then, the student team was ready. With the help of our interpreter, the students presented the gospel over and over, through puppets, music, drama, dance and testimony. Everything that a YWAM team could have in its arsenal was used that afternoon to make the message clear. Some of the children were frightened by the strange little faces that rose above the puppeteer's curtain, but they were soon laughing and responding to their new fabric friends, like children everywhere. The school's presentation ended as Greg Dryden, an architect from New Zealand, stood to share a powerful message about his own efforts to find peace in empty hopes apart from God and the answer he had found in Jesus Christ.

To conclude, I rose to speak. I could feel all eyes on me as the crowd waited expectantly for me to speak and Harry to interpret. "I am honored that you fly the flag of my home country." I paused for Harry to translate.

"But as an American, I can tell you that we have had to learn that we cannot put our hope in America. We cannot wait for America to help us. We have many problems in America, but we have learned to put our hope and trust in Jesus Christ. He is the only answer to our problems. He is the only assurance of joy and peace and eternal life."

The islanders listened intently as I continued, silently asking God to help me simply communicate His message in a format relevant to their lives. "You do not have to wait for Jesus to come, because He has always been here. Jesus came to show us how to live. He came to die for us so that we could go to heaven to live with Him....We have come from all over the world to bring this message to you. We have given you the message from God."

Since I had arranged earlier to meet with the chiefs at the conclusion of our program, I finished by saying, "I know that your chiefs are wise men. I know that they care about you. I can tell because you have such a fine village. We will now meet with your chiefs to see whether there is anything more that we can do to help you."

As the villagers and team members began to disperse and visit with one another, I asked Gary Peters, Diane Hetfield, Harry and Pastor Willy to accompany me as I walked with the dozen or so chiefs to the John Frum headquarters. We approached the area where the American and U.S. Navy flags were flying and then turned to duck into the small doorway of the headquarters, where we sat crowded on woven mats covering the dirt floors of the thatched room.

The headquarters is the well-maintained heart of the John Frum village. Along one low wall, a number of old military jackets and helmets were carefully hanging. Lining another low wall were the red-tipped bamboo sticks that are the villagers' makeshift bayonet rifles. The men of the village customarily march in military fashion, wearing their bits of uniforms with USA painted in red across their chests or backs and carrying the bamboo bayonets around their parade grounds. Keeping the military customs alive is an important way of staying true to John Frum. On the wall opposite the entrance, a placard with the names of the various villages along with other flags and symbols of the movement hangs above a table with a small American flag in the center.

Chief Isaak One and I sat on the ground near the table, and before I could say a word, Isaak requested, "Please, send someone to teach us and to help us."

I was surprised to hear such an open request from a man who had just two days earlier said that he wasn't interested in Jesus or the church. I wanted to clarify his request. I said, "I am a Christian missionary. I come in the name of Jesus Christ. I offer help through the gospel of Jesus Christ."

Isaak said, "I know you are a Christian missionary. Please send someone to teach us and to help us."

Since I was not sure whether I was understanding our interpreter properly, I pressed further. "If I am able to find someone who would come here, would you let them say whatever they want to say, give them an English-speaking person to interpret for them and give them a place to live?"

"Yes," Isaak replied sincerely. And then the man who had earned his name by saying things only once repeated for the third time, "Please, send someone to teach us and to help us."

I took a deep breath and then looked straight into the chief's eyes. "Tomorrow I will go home to New Zealand and then to the United States, and I will see whether I can find someone who will come."

Chief Isaak One rose from the mat and stooped slightly as he left the John Frum headquarters. I glanced at Harry, my interpreter, who motioned for me to stay put. Soon the chief returned to his place, sitting cross-legged on the mat, carrying a collection of five colorful woven baskets.

The baskets were about the size of a purse, with two long, braided ties that joined together at the ends to form a carrying strap. They are commonly used by the Tannese men and women to carry personal belongings. On a Pacific island, where everything from the floor mats to the roofs is made of woven vegetation, these baskets were clearly works of art. Isaak graciously offered them to me as a gift, suggesting I could take them home for my wife to use to carry her things. Gift giving is a very important part of relationship building and sealing negotiations in the Pacific. I had always made it a habit to have gift items with me for occasions like this. I flushed as I realized that I had been so nervous about the day's activities that I had forgotten to prepare any gifts. I received the baskets with my best composure while I searched my mind and the possessions of my associates in the room for anything I might permanently borrow for a gift! I could not believe I had come so unprepared. I had deliberately traveled light, with only my pocket Bible and my passport safely buttoned in my right front shirt pocket, just in case I needed to get off the island in a hurry!

Suddenly I felt my hand reaching into my pocket for my little leather-bound Bible. I could hardly believe what I was doing. I loved this Bible! I had used it for nearly ten years to read and preach from in all different settings. It was my favorite, and we had been so many places together. If I had taken time to prepare a proper gift, it would probably not have been a Bible, and certainly not my little Bible.

But I knew something was compelling me to present this gift to Isaak. I pulled the well-used New American Standard Bible from my shirt pocket and held it gently in my hands. I glanced at it one last time as I held it out to Isaak and said, "This is my gift for you…" My words nearly choked in my throat as I noticed that all the printed titles from the cover and spine of the Bible had long ago been worn off, leaving only one word engraved in gold on the front of the Bible—my first name, John.

I hesitated as I thought, "Oh, no, this is not a good gift!" I remembered too that the inside cover bore my name and my old address in California, USA. This could play right into their mythology: John from America's book! But in the middle of my frantic thoughts I felt God say, "It's okay, this is the perfect gift."

The chief was looking at me. I held out my Bible and continued. "This is my gift for you, my friend. It is a very special book. God gave us this book because He loves us. In this book, God tells us how to be good chiefs. He tells us how to get along with each other. And He tells us about His son Jesus, who came to us to show us how to live and to die for us so that we can all go to heaven together. If you get one of your English-speaking people to explain this book to you, you can learn about these things. I have read and taught from this Bible for many years, and now I am giving it to you."

The chief reverently took the Bible with both hands and said, "I know this is a holy book. And I know that the help you offer is on the basis of this book. Please, send someone to teach us and to help us."

I felt as if I were in a dream. My mind reflected on the many missionary contact stories I had read. I was humbled as I thought about the magnitude of what God was doing here and now. I realized that I had been under the impression that this kind of thing—breakthroughs to unreached peoples—had all been done already. I had certainly never envisioned playing a part in this kind of work. I felt very inept for the job. So many people and their eternities might depend on this moment. What was I supposed to do now?

SEVEN

"Please Send Someone"

WE said our farewells and gathered the team into the vans. Harry announced, "The chief has given you permission to take all of your people up to the volcano."

I thanked Isaak One, shaking his hand, and then climbed into the van. We waved good-bye as we began the excursion to the top of Yasur. The vans were able to follow a road around and up the mountain to an area about three hundred meters from the volcano's rim. My heart pounded on the steep slope as the delicate ash and cinders crunched beneath my feet. Slowly, we ascended toward the angry sounds and thick smoke that billowed over the rim ahead of us. Reaching the brink of the crater, we pensively peered into the fiery bowl and flirted with the unstable edge of the cone. There are no guardrails here. Others have fallen in and perished as their footing has given way. I was not eager to see whether or not John from America really could survive the inside of this volcano!

The fiery display was awesome and mesmerizing as plumes and explosions of red-hot lava and burning gas leapt from the molten depths. Waves of hot, sulfurous gas stung our eyes and made breathing both difficult and unpleasant. Sometimes the volcano is so active that it would be impossible to be so near. Locals speak of how they have lit their cigarettes on the glowing cinders that land around them on the rim. It is quite easy to see how the villagers would come to read the mood of their gods by listening to and gazing at the "fiery voice." We watched with fascination, taking photos and videos, but the incredible scene only added to the surreal feeling that had been with me from the beginning of the week's events.

Soon we grew uncomfortable with our proximity to the molten chaos and began our retreat to the vans below. As we descended, I looked out over the varied island topography. To the left was the austere, ashen plain containing Lake Siwi's obsidian dark reflection. On the right lay the verdant valley that led to the village tapestry and glittering beach of Sulphur Bay. The tiny village huts were easily seen. I paused to pray for this special community and its courageous leader who had made a bold decision to allow a new message, a new set of values and a new God for his people. The chief surely knew that as the church was allowed to work in his villages, its influence would grow and the chief of "John Frum" might well become the chief of no one.

I prayed that God would use the events of the day, whether they were providence or folly, to bring these wonderful people to Christ. I asked for wisdom as to how to proceed. In a moment of utter reverence, I removed one of my flower leis and placed it over a rugged wooden post that jutted out from the cinder slopes. I stepped back to view the lifeless post now covered with beautiful flowers, set against the sky above and the village below. It was a moment of dedication for me. "Use me however You wish to fulfill Your vision for these people, O God. I don't know what this may mean, but I entrust myself to You."

That evening, we discussed the day's events in an informal meeting. I urged everyone to keep the matter to himself. We realized that it would be in no one's best interest to publicize the matter just yet. Time would tell whether this was a genuine breakthrough. If it was, it would be good to give the people some time to work the issues out before much attention was brought to bear on the matter. I also knew that it would be important for me to return to see how the dust had settled from these events and to keep my relationship with the chief and others growing. But for now, after this last very draining week of many away from home, I was ready to pack my things, go to bed and fly home the following day.

The pastors who had attended the seminar presented a great celebration meal after the final Friday morning session. We rejoiced over the developments of the past week. As we exchanged speeches, I emphasized the need for churches to work together to reach out to the John Frum and kastom people on the island. Pacific churches are not known for cooperation across denominational lines. This conference and the other Mercy Ship activities had been the first time that these barriers had come down, if only slightly, and I wanted to encourage these leaders in their efforts to see their common ground and goals.

Throughout the week, my background and status as a nondenominational pastor were fascinating to the other pastors, who were surprised to hear of my work with a variety of churches. The fact that the Mercy Ship's American director named John was a pastor who had spent a week speaking to a consortium of island church leaders no doubt sent a forceful message to the John Frum community about my strong connection to the church and about the church's acceptance of John. If the John Frum people were going to be evangelized, it would be through the growing acceptance and cooperation of tribal and church leaders. I realized that my persona represented a mediatorial union of John Frum expectations and the Christian message. I wanted to see that both of these parties went forward with wisdom and goodwill.

Pastor Willy impressed me when he remarked, "Pastor John, we can't go into Sulphur Bay and take down their flag. John Frum is a part of their life and culture. We need to slowly work together, to build trust, to see that they put their faith in Jesus, and John Frum will be put in the right place." This island Presbyterian leader was sensitive to the fact that none of us would appreciate having our national flag and cultural identity erased by our church. In the past, this had been the reality faced by so many non-Western cultures as Christianity made its way around the globe. Modern missions is struggling to learn how to complement the new cultures it encounters, introducing Jesus in His rightful, relevant way.

I was never more ready to come home from anywhere as I was that afternoon when my local friends put me on the small plane. The plane rumbled down the rolling grass strip and into the air. I was overjoyed to be home with Shari and our children. However, after spending a week as a near-deity island figure, my treatment was a bit of a letdown. Shari, weary of long, demanding days alone, quickly asked me to take out the rubbish and clean up after the children. No respect, I thought! But it was great to be home.

In the meantime, the *Ruby* teams were finishing up the rest of their work on Tanna. By the time the ship departed for Fiji, the dental teams had treated over two hundred patients and distributed 150 dental health kits to island children. The optometry clinic had examined and provided eyeglasses for more than six hundred people, and the medical doctors had made rounds covering much of the island. The ship's engineers had successfully repaired one of the hospital's water tanks and had restored its only ambulance to working condition. That story was a miracle in itself, as the ambulance had been broken down for years. A passing coffee plantation owner saw the *Ruby's* engineers working on the old Land Rover and asked what the problem was. The engineers explained that the vehicle's rusty fuel pump somewhat resembled a sieve. The man mentioned that he had an old, dilapidated Land Rover sitting on his nearby property. He told the engineers that they were welcome to use any spare parts they needed. It just so happened that of all the rusted, unsalvageable parts the engineers discovered on the man's Land Rover, the one part they found to be in working order was the fuel pump, which fit perfectly on the old ambulance, restoring it to the hospital's service!

The morning the *Ruby* was scheduled to depart, a large island thank-you feast was held in Lenakel for the ship's crew. Whole roasted pig and goat along with a myriad of roasted and boiled roots and tubers, rice and fruits were set out on a long table. When the plates ran out, large, green multipurpose leaves were stacked at the end of the table for the crew's use. After the hearty feast came the traditional singing, handshaking and presentation of gifts. Every crew member received woven fans, baskets, colorful grass skirts or beautifully carved walking sticks. Each female crew member was also presented with a hand-sewn multicolored Mother Hubbard dress, the common cloth-ing worn by the island women. There was plenty for everyone as a show of gratitude for the gifts of healing and hope that we had brought to their island. The festivities were not over yet. A large group of men wearing grass skirts and lava-lavas gathered in a circle and began a tra-ditional island dance, stomping the ground and slapping their hands and skin in a rhythmic, crescendoing beat. Then, in the distance, the sound of singing was heard. Slowly, a procession of colorfully clad island men came into view, walking in single file, carrying what appeared to be a very heavy load fastened onto a long, wooden pole. The pole was supported horizontally across the shoulders of several men. As the group neared, the amazed crew recognized what the men were carrying: a seven-foot-long boat made of fruit, fashioned in the likeness of the *Pacific Ruby*! The crew joined in the march as the heav-ily laden fruit boat was carried all the way to the ship across the nar-row gangway and placed carefully on the deck, suspended between two adjacent railings.

After thanking their island friends and lashing the fruit boat securely to the railings, the deck crew hauled in the gangway and released the mooring lines. Captain Jesse maneuvered the vessel care-fully away from the dock, once again covered with Tannese well-wishers waving and singing their hymns of farewell. The crew members lined the railings to say good-bye, many dressed in their newly received Mother Hubbard dresses, as beautifully sung refrains of "God be with you till we meet again" drifted over the ocean waves. We always leave a place feeling like we have received much more than we have given.

Back in New Zealand, I was constantly aware of Chief Isaak's request. His repeated appeal to "please send someone" played over and over in my mind. What was I going to do now?

I spent the next weeks researching the John Frum movement and trying to understand what had transpired during my short stay in Tanna. The more I thought about it, the more certain I was that it must have all been a rather extraordinary dream. My wife and children stared blankly at me as I tried to convince them of what I had just experienced. Thankfully, my research confirmed that these people did indeed exist and, furthermore, that their history included myriads of convoluted tales all centered around an American named John. I wasn't sure whether this made me feel any better or not.

I kept coming back to the same question. Why me, Lord? I don't believe in coincidence. My mind was having trouble once again understanding one of the greatest mysteries of the universe—why does a sovereign, almighty God choose to work in such mysterious ways? More so, why does He choose such unlikely characters as He writes the pages of history?

My personal background could easily be used to prove that God has a humorous side! As a youth, my disdain of Christianity compelled me to start an atheist club dedicated to antagonizing those we deemed to be "religious." My parents had long been disillusioned with the Church. My father was an atheist, and although my mother had been raised in a Reformed church, she had drifted from her faith and upbringing. My parents were well-educated, both being schoolteachers in Daly City, California. My father possessed a significant knowledge of math and science which he passed on to me along with the firm belief that the Christian Church had nearly ruined the world and that science was in the process of bringing us a happier existence. Evolutionary thinking was on the uprise, and religion was, happily, declining.

I can remember sitting on the back porch of our home, stacked on the side of a hill, as was typical of the old San Francisco area neighborhoods of that day. Our neighbors were Catholic, and their children had come over to play with me and my younger brother Bart. As they innocently began to talk about church and God, I jumped right in and told them that God didn't exist. Scientists had proven evolution, and any other belief showed an extreme lack of intelligence!

My mother cautioned me one day after the neighborhood parents complained about her son's ungodly influence on their children. She explained that I should not be so vocal in expressing my opinions. I thought that she was being wishy-washy and was not willing to stand up for important values!

One of the highlights of my youth was being a Scout. During my Cub Scout days, I can remember looking forward every year to the Pinewood Derby! Each boy was given a block of pine along with a set of plastic wheels and premade axles. Our job was to whittle the wood into the shape of a car and attach the axles and wheels. The great climax was the day of the race, when our cars were judged on appearance and then raced down a gravity track. Many of the entries were beautiful! Some were near perfect replicas of classic models of the time. Some even had leather upholstered seats and steering wheels. Clearly the boys' fathers had helped them by using expensive woodworking tools and equipment. Our father, on the other hand, had taught Bart and me to shave the wood down until only a thin sliver of a car remained. Then we carved out the inside and melted Dad's lead fishing weights and poured the liquid inside. We painstakingly sanded everything and finally applied a high-gloss lacquer paint. Without realizing it, Bart and I were being taught basic physics lessons. I remember the jeers and harassment I often received for the truly ugly appearance of my cars. Although I never won the beauty contest, I always went home with a trophy from the race.

Experiences like that shaped my viewpoint, reinforcing my parents' teaching that what is on the inside is more important than outward appearances. I learned this lesson well, even to an almost detrimental level. As I grew older, I found myself drawn to things and people out of the mainstream. I often found myself not feeling like part of the crowd. My mother took me aside and explained, "John, if the majority of the people are doing it, it's probably wrong. The best way to live, act and think is not always the most popular way." So I found myself feeling compelled to be different, to somehow distinguish myself from my peers. This became a double-edged sword. It helped me avoid much of the peer pressure I saw others being sucked into, but it also led me to seek the company of people not accepted by the mainstream of society. I took great pride in being different and not caring about what other people thought of me.

All throughout my childhood and adolescence, during summer breaks from school, my parents would load up our camping gear and take us on extended trips all over the United States and Canada. My parents were inclined to travel and explore, always employing simple and modest means. Their attraction to a more rural lifestyle, combined with their growing concern over my peer group, motivated them to make inquiries into teaching positions available in the mountain communities some two and one-half hours east of San Francisco. The myriad communities in the foothills of the Sierra Nevada were full of historical ambiance from their gold-mining roots, and my dad, being quite the history buff, was drawn to these gold rush towns.

My parents also were concerned about the growing suburban danger posed by the drug culture in Daly City and the San Francisco Bay Area. They wanted to provide a more wholesome environment for their sons. I had become prone to troublemaking and was spending more and more time with an undesirable crowd. So it happened that when I was twelve, my parents purchased an isolated twelve-acre property in the historic gold rush community of San Andreas. Our only neighbors were horses and cows, and my only playmate was my younger brother by a year and a half. I was unaware that in these very hills I too would discover "gold."

PART TWO

"Are Atheists Going to Church?"

EIGHT

There's Gold in Them Thar Hills!

IN moving to San Andreas, my parents had pursued the golden dream of a more peaceful life. The staff of my new junior high school, however, found their peace suddenly disrupted upon my arrival. I was an undesirable student, frequently in trouble and skillful at involving others in my mischief. I continued to be bored by academics, with one exception. My math and science teacher was a disciplined, intelligent man who created a challenging and inviting learning environment. I was fascinated by science, and my young mind was captivated by TV shows like *Star Trek* and the emerging U.S. space program. It was a time when scientific pursuits were highly esteemed. Science and technology were coming to the forefront in the midst of the humanistic era, sexual revolution and all the movements that were shifting the focus away from traditional values.

During our final year of junior high, my class was given an orientation to the local high school. It was explained to us that secondary school was the "real world," where a lot would be expected of us and we would have to work hard. We were told that at the end of our high school years, the top two students would receive a special award and be allowed to give a speech at the graduation ceremony. I was intrigued by this idea. I wanted to have that honor and address my fellow classmates and teachers. I don't know whether it was the emerging preacher in me or whether I just wanted the opportunity to tell everyone my opinion of their education system, but I set that as my seemingly unobtainable goal. I realized that to be given that platform, I would have to be one of the top two students. I also realized that everyone else had quite a head start on me academically. I knew that if I did well in high school, I could go on to do whatever I wanted. Whether I went to university or decided to be a beach bum, doing well in high school would greatly increase my options for later life.

And then there was Barbara! Barbara and I rode the school bus together. She was a fantastic student and very intelligent girl, and I had become quite infatuated with her. My desire to impress her, along with my tenacity to reach my goal, propelled me through an extremely difficult first year of high school. For the first time, I had to learn how to behave, study and take tests. My discipline was rewarded by the second and third quarters of my first high school year, when I began to receive good grades and even rank in the top of the class. My passion for science and math blossomed, and my teachers began to take an interest in me, becoming my mentors and friends.

Early in my high school years, I was affected by another television drama called *Medical Center*. I decided that I wanted to go into medicine and become a doctor. My parents and teachers were thrilled with my decision and proudly helped me toward my new goal.

My commitment to science and knowledge was unwavering, as was my disdain for Christianity. The Jesus Movement, a particularly troubling movement for a committed atheist such as I, had been growing in popularity. I was especially disturbed and angered by the presence of special campus groups like Campus Life. People were taking such an interest in God and Jesus. There were church-related youth groups targeting high school campuses like ours. All of these factors caused me to become more and more militant and outspoken about my atheistic beliefs. I gathered like-minded friends around me and discussed ways to discourage religious movements that were growing on our campus. We sarcastically formed our own atheists' group. Wanting to mock Christianity, we developed our own religion called "Butterflyism" and even wrote a "Butterfly bible." We claimed to worship "The Great Butterfly" and would disrupt class with mock appearances of our over-sized insect. I was the self-appointed, acknowledged head of the group and the only member truly committed to our atheistic agenda. Behind all the spoof was a serious effort on my part to engage Christians in conversation and talk them out of their beliefs or discredit them in any way I could.

A principal character in my life at that time was Vernon Mayhall, the pastor of the local Assembly of God church and an aggressive, com-munity-oriented man. Vernon was also our area Boy Scout leader. Bart and I had joined the local Boy Scout troop when we moved to San Andreas and participated actively in all the related activities. Vernon was not overpowering when sharing his opinions, but he certainly made his beliefs clear, particularly at Boy Scout campfires. I was a jun-ior camp leader and was disturbed that our Scout master was obviously using the campouts and evenings around the campfire as a platform to sell his religion and explain his archaic beliefs. I did my best to object to his subtle lectures and always devoted myself to taking equal time to make it clear that there was no longer a need for such nonscientific reli-gious babble. While Vernon was long-suffering, he also made it clear that I would not be able to receive the Eagle award, Scouting's highest rank, as long as I persisted as an atheist. He pointed out that the last of the twelve Scout laws was to be "reverent." I was disappointed to miss out on this, my next and long-worked-for rank, but I was also pleased to be taking a stand against Scouting's emphasis on God.

Despite the tension in our relationship, Vernon recommended that I represent our Scouting district by participating in the Northern California delegation troop to the 13th World Scouting Jamboree in 1971. This global gathering of select Scouts happens every four years and is a high honor to attend. We were encamped with twenty-eight thousand delegates from all over the world on the slopes of Japan's majestic and sacred dormant volcano, Mount Fujiyama. The rolling landscape was covered as far as the eye could see with the orderly arrangements of thousands of multicolored tents and troops flying the flag of their homeland. Eagle Scout Neil Armstrong had only recently returned from the moon and was the keynote speaker on this grand occasion.

Within days, the jamboree was tragically disrupted by a fierce and dangerous typhoon that led to a chaotic emergency evacuation of the camp. The terrifying scene drove the young crowd to an everyone-for-himself mentality that was a stark and distressing departure from the lofty ideals that Scouts are supposed to represent. Long after my return home, I was still troubled by the thought of how readily our baser instincts could take control in spite of all our laws and pledges.

My personal moral disquiet was renewed the following summer. Before my final year of high school, I was accepted by a nearby college to study chemistry, and I stayed with a family friend who lived in a spacious A-frame house in the mountains near the college. I quickly discovered I was in for an eye-opening summer. The friend was a certified hippie whose house was always open to her many friends in the drug culture. I was shocked by the amoral behavior and declined participation in any of the household activities. I frequently wondered whether the police would show up at any minute and haul us all to jail. I could imagine the headlines proclaiming that a high school honor student had been among the rabble arrested! My observation led me into much thought about moral values. I wondered why I embraced the values that I did—is there a real basis in natural law for a moral code?

I returned to San Andreas shortly before my senior year of high school began. I was eager to see Barbara. We had become very good friends and dated occasionally. Just one year earlier, to my utter astonishment and dismay, Barbara had become a Christian! I had argued incessantly with her, trying to bring her back to her senses. I could not understand why she had become a Christian! She was a brilliant girl, and I knew her well. Often after a date I would accompany her to her parents' kitchen, where she would prepare hot cocoa and ask me pointed questions about spiritual matters. I would patiently listen as she read books about faith to me, and even portions of the Bible. She challenged me to read Jesus' Sermon on the Mount, and I was undeniably impressed with the incredible ethic that Jesus had so simply communicated.

This night, after my summer away, Barbara was talking about miracles. I became exasperated telling her she had once been so smart but now she had apparently said good-bye to her brains, believing in the medieval idea of miracles! She angrily retorted, "John Rush! You're studying science and biology—isn't life a miracle?!!"

Barbara later did not remember saying those words, but it was a sentence I would never forget. It was only a few days before school was to start. I sat cloistered in my bedroom, coming out only for meals. My mind was spinning. I thought about science. Humankind had figured out atoms, figured out the vastness of space—everything from the humongous to the minuscule—but what about life? What about beauty and personality, friendship and creativity. What about love? Life is so diverse, and it didn't have to be! What about flowers? It was like the world was meant to be seen. It is beautiful and pleasant; it doesn't just fulfill an evolutionary purpose. Barbara was right—life is a miracle! I could not explain this complexity as a product of random process. Even as the great evolutionary astrophysicist Sir Fred Hoyle was forced to admit, "A common sense interpretation of the facts suggests that a superintellect has monkeyed with physics, as well as with chemistry and biology, and that there are no blind forces worth speaking about in nature."

After three days in my room pondering these things, having never been to a church service or taught a "sinner's prayer," I simply looked out my window and said, "Okay, You win. I have been wrong." I directed this prayer to the God of the Bible that Barbara had been telling me about. I had no idea what to do next, but I didn't want to tell anyone what I had done. I wanted to see whether something different would happen.

The following day was our first day of school. Barbara was already on the bus, saving me a seat. We chatted, but I avoided any discussion of spiritual things. That day at school, I was amazed not by any external difference in myself but by an internal change. I was unmistakably aware of a moral compass in me that had not been there before. I sensed a supernatural presence in me, guiding my thoughts and convicting me of wrong attitudes and actions. For me, this was a clear witness of the reality of God in my life.

After school, I boarded the bus home and once again sat next to Barbara. As the bus came to my stop, I looked at Barbara and pointed to the big Bible on her lap. I said, "Oh, by the way, I let Him in last night." As the bus pulled away, Barbara struggled to get the window down and hung her head out to yell back to me, "John Rush!! What do you mean? Call me!"

Confessing my newfound faith to Barbara was easy in comparison with telling the rest of my friends. Our atheists' group was scheduled to meet for its first session of the year, with me presiding. I stood up before virtually all of the friends I had and announced that I would no longer be able to serve as the leader of the group because I had discovered that the Christians were right and we were wrong. They were shocked as I explained that I too had become a believer. My proclamation caused quite a stir, and I lost most of the people I considered to be my friends.

I had to face my arch rival, Pastor Vernon Mayhall, as well. After our Scout meeting, I approached Vernon and asked what time his church met on Sundays. He was plainly surprised and asked, "What, are atheists going to church now?" He was puzzled and a bit cautious but told me their service started at eleven o'clock.

That Sunday, I dug an old white leather Bible out of our family library. The Bible belonged to my mother but had long since fallen into disuse. Throughout the service, Pastor Mayhall watched me curiously. He had little reason to expect I had become a Christian and every reason to expect I was trying to expand my attempts at foiling his evangelistic efforts. At the end of the service, the altar call was given and I went forward. I shared in front of the entire congregation, many of whom knew me well and were amazed, that I had given my heart and life to Jesus.

As difficult as it had been to confess my faith to my friends, to Pastor Mayhall and even to the entire congregation, telling my family proved to be the hardest of all. My father was very upset. I was as inclined as ever to share my opinions and relentlessly pointed out my father's need to get right with God. I was very immature in the handling of my faith and our relationship. My father thought I had lost my mind and in anger disowned me. Our relationship became more and more estranged as I spent all of my time at church and Boy Scouts. The one remaining glimmer of hope in my father's eyes was my devotion to school and preparation for premedical studies.

I had applied to the University of the Pacific and planned to attend its bilingual school. I was the leader of our school's foreign language club. My parents and instructors were trying to adjust to the fact that I had become a "Jesus Freak" but thought at least I was still planning to go into medicine, to do well in university and distinguish myself. A lot of pride and hopes were fixed on me by my teachers, mentors and parents. I was soon to be awarded scholarships and the top award for science and mathematics from my high school. I would graduate tied for third place academically. I was delighted that Barbara had finished in first place and had earned the honor of addressing our graduating class!

Then God, on Easter Sunday of that year, began speaking to me. I had been away from school for the week of spring break, and I had received my letter of acceptance from the University of the Pacific. Quite frankly, I wasn't interested in hearing from God and was committed to my own ambitions. After the Sunday service, I went for a walk around our twelve-acre farm. I gazed at the wildflowers and wandered through the green spring grass, asking God what was on His mind. I was finally ready to hear what He had been trying to say to me. God began to point out the fields of waving green grass. He said, "John, I want you to work in My harvest as a pastor." I was not excited to hear this. I explained that nobody would like this idea, including me! God said, "You don't have to do this, but I want you to…and I want your answer today." I thought, "Why?! Are you going to ask somebody else to do this job if I decline??" I remember later that day reading my Bible. I always marked the date on the page next to where I started my daily reading. That day I wrote the word *yes* next to the date in the margin. That was my simple yes to God to lay down my own ambitions and study to be a pastor.

Hell broke loose. My parents were appalled, furious! They refused to support my education if I was studying to be a pastor. My teachers were stunned. There was even talk between my dad and my teachers about having me deprogrammed. I rethought my decision time after time, trying to talk myself and God out of it. I always came back to that simple yes to follow Jesus. My decision further alienated me from my family, except my brother, who had seen the true change in me and had also become a Christian. We became allies, supporting each other.

Many would disagree with us, but we knew that we had discovered a true treasure in these hills worth far more than all the precious metal ever found here!

NINE

"Your Dad Is Ill"

M Y family was still reeling over my announcement to give up my pursuit of medicine in favor of becoming a pastor. I had approached Pastor Mayhall and told him that God wanted me to go into the ministry and that my parents were going to kill me and that I was holding him personally responsible for the whole thing! He responded by making me an associate pastor in his church and allowing me to preach on Sunday nights! I was completely terror-stricken by this idea. I had been a Christian only about six months. I had no background in Christianity and knew very little about the Bible. Suddenly public speaking held no appeal whatsoever. Additionally, Pastor Mayhall gave me a Sunday school class to teach. My young students had to help me locate books and stories in the Bible!

I couldn't afford to go to Bible college, so I attended general education classes at Delta Community College in Stockton, a town about an hour away. I rented an apartment nearby for the first quarter but soon moved back to San Andreas and rented the small house that I had helped my parents build on our farm years earlier. I remained enrolled at Delta, riding the bus there and back every day. I continued in my role as an assistant pastor at the church throughout that year, teaching a Sunday school class and preaching the Sunday evening services.

Pastor Mayhall invited me to attend a seminar on creationism given by scientists who were Christians. The book of Genesis seemed to be an incredible fairy tale to me, and my attempts to reconcile it with everything I "knew" about evolutionary science had frustrated me endlessly. I was amused that Pastor Mayhall would think that there were real scientists who could actually believe the creation story! I agreed to attend but was very doubtful and wary. I listened with fascination as pioneers in the realm of creation science one by one ruined my arguments as an evolutionist and validated the Genesis story. I was converted to creationism and voraciously read every book and article I could find on the subject. I was soon asked by local churches, youth groups and even my old high school to speak on creationism. I had many lively debates with my former teachers and mentors. I was even invited to debate professors at California State University in front of their science classes. Winning these debates proved easy when even prominent evolutionists admit, "The absence of fossil evidence for intermediate stages between major transitions in organic design…has been a persistent and nagging problem."[1]

The following year, my parents had a change of heart and decided that if their son wanted to go to Bible school, it was better than not pursuing further education at all, and so they made it possible for me to attend Bethany Bible College. Even though Bethany was nearly three hours from San Andreas, I often came home on weekends to preach at church and visit friends and family.

Upon arrival at Bethany, everyone had to take a test of his biblical knowledge. In contrast to my junior high days, tests were no longer a problem for me. I had scored in the high percentiles in aptitude tests for state university entrance. Now, however, I was competing against people who had grown up in Sunday schools. I scored in the eleventh percentile and was humiliated! Literature and history were not my strengths! The year went quickly, and I made many new friends, including a young woman named Shari Hanson, from nearby San Jose. Shari and I worked together in the cafeteria throughout the term and began a lifelong friendship.

By the end of the year, my biblical illiteracy had earned me a lower than normal grade point average. I returned to San Andreas for the summer, resuming my role at the church and working for my former physics teacher in his growing construction business. By the time fall arrived and the school year was about to begin, I was faced with a difficult choice. I wished to continue my education, but Pastor Mayhall was in ill health, and I was needed at the church. I also had a good job, so I decided to postpone my return to college until the spring term. That spring, I did return to school, but this time to Biola University in Southern California. I was in for quite an experience!

I happened to meet the leader of the campus preaching ministry who invited me to join him. He had organized evangelistic meetings in the war-torn gang center of East Los Angeles. I was shaken as we drove up and down the streets where homes were filled with bullet holes and murals depicted police officers and rival gang members who'd been killed. Drugs were sold openly on the streets. Our guide was a former heroine dealer in the area. My first opportunity to preach was in a school auditorium. I had prepared a sermon, but as I looked at the audience I tossed my notes under my chair and apprehensively approached the platform. I felt totally incapable and intimidated and delivered the shortest sermon of my life! I said honestly that I could not imagine the problems they had to face, but I knew that Jesus could. He was the answer for me, and I knew that He was the answer for them. I invited all who wanted to pray or talk about their problems to come forward. I expected to sit down quickly and leave soon. To my surprise, there was a large response. Our counselors began to pray with people one by one. Soon a rough-looking character approached me. He was crying and wanted to talk to me. I asked him why he was so upset, and he replied that he had "hit" eleven people. In my ignorance, it took me a minute to figure out that this man meant he had been paid to kill eleven people. My time at Biola gave me a greater understanding of the hardships of inner-city life in America.

I returned to San Andreas to find that Pastor Mayhall's physical condition had worsened. After much consideration, I decided to stay in San Andreas and assist with the mounting work at the church. I found a job as a school bus driver and rented a small storefront area that I converted into a community coffeehouse with a room at the back where I lived. Members of our church donated furnishings for the coffeehouse and prepared food to serve to patrons. The Koinonia Coffee House, named after the Greek word for fellowship, became a thriving ministry to students and down-and-outers in San Andreas.

In November of that year, I received a disquieting phone call. My mom had just found my dad lying unconscious in the kitchen. My dad had apparently fallen and was now recovering on the sofa. My mom asked me to come over and sit with Dad while she ran some errands. I arrived to find my father lying on the sofa with a bucket nearby. He was still feeling quite nauseated and had a severe headache. He said he had been standing near the fireplace mantle when he was hit with an acute pain in his head. He had made it into the kitchen before passing out. I remember sitting in an armchair, chatting superficially with my dad for several minutes. Despite the years, the tension between us had not lessened. I don't even remember what we discussed that day. I had no idea those words would be the last normal conversation I would ever have with my father. Even as we spoke, irreversible damage was taking place through blood and fluid coming in contact with the surface of his brain. My dad was suffering from a ruptured cerebral aneurysm. The brain's natural protective response is to close off capillaries to restrain bleeding, consequently starving portions of itself.

In the following hours, as Dad's condition grew worse, we admitted him to the local hospital. Dad was eventually transferred to the larger hospital in Stockton an hour and a half away. The doctors there were the first to properly diagnose my dad as having suffered a stroke. They performed CAT scans, which revealed the amount of damage being done. By this time, however, my father had slipped into a comatose state. I felt emotionally numb throughout the experience. After a few days, we returned to San Andreas, leaving Dad at St. Joseph's Hospital.

Our family endured the holiday season with little joy. Dad had lingered in a coma for six weeks. My mother's time was torn between staying near Dad in the hospital and returning home to manage her vacant household. One afternoon, she called to say that Bart and I needed to take her to the hospital. The doctors had called and said they didn't expect Dad to make it through the night. I hung up the phone. The numb feeling was still there. I was suddenly struck by the fact that I hadn't shed a tear over my father's sickness. The years of tension had hardened my heart toward my dad. I closed my eyes, praying to my heavenly Father. "Lord, this isn't right! You love my dad. He's been a good man, a good father. Please help me to be able to cry!" As I prayed, slowly I began to weep and be filled with compassion for my father. Finally I found myself crying out to God to spare his life and give him another chance. "He doesn't know You yet!" Suddenly, I remembered a dream I had had shortly after my conversion. In this dream, my dad had become a Christian. I was immediately overcome with a most remarkable feeling. I was completely assured that my father would not die and that he would inexplicably come out of his coma.

Bart and his wife, Tina, drove Mom and me to Stockton. I sat in the back with my mom and pondered how I could comfort her with the assurance that God had given me. Finally I said, "Mom, I believe God has shown me that Dad won't die but he'll come out of the coma." My mother became distraught and asked me how I could bring up my religion at a time like this. She admonished me that we had to come to grips with the fact that we were about to lose Dad and that we had to let him go. The rest of the ride was very quiet.

On entering my dad's hospital room, I stared at all of the apparatus hooked up to his body that was keeping him alive. The sound of the respirator punctuated the silence. I remembered all the campouts, all the fun times, all the hard times, all the pain—all wrapped up in that one moment. I told my dad how much I loved him and then said good-bye and left the room. Mom remained at the hospital through the night, but I stayed at a hotel. The next morning as Bart, Tina and I returned to the hospital, we were met before we reached the front door by Mom, smiling! She was excitedly speaking to us. "You'll never believe it! The doctors say he's had a miraculous turnaround in the night and he's going to be okay. He's going to make it through!" It was a vital moment for my mother, rekindling her childhood faith. Before long we were moving Mom and Dad into their new home, a small apartment they rented in Stockton to be near the hospital and clinics.

The whole family gathered for dinner to welcome Dad home. The stroke had paralyzed his right side and destroyed the speech center in his brain. As we all began to partake of our meals, my father clearly objected. Unable to talk, he held up his left hand and motioned as if clasping two hands in prayer. He uttered the sounds, "Bray, bray!" We were astonished by his simple words. Dad used to make it clear that our family would not say grace at the table! Now he was asking us to pray. Over the course of time, we discovered that Dad had had some sort of encounter with Jesus. Not long after that, my mother called to say that Dad wanted to see me. During our visit, Dad seemed anxious to communicate something to me. As he struggled to speak, I slowly realized that what he sorely wanted was simply to apologize for all the hard times. Our reconciliation brought the entire family into the Christian faith.

TEN

Naked in the Hall

I T is in the midst of our greatest struggles that God brings our greatest blessings. With Dad in the hospital, Christmas of 1976 had been less than festive. Pastor Mayhall was still ill, and I was keeping particularly busy filling numerous roles as an assistant pastor at our church. It was time for a few days off! The day after Christmas, I jumped into my little red truck and set off for Stockton. I had two objectives. One was to visit my dad in the hospital, and the second was to register for night classes at Delta College. I had been continuing my education by correspondence, taking a New Testament Greek course.

As I reached the city limits, I noticed that the red oil light on my dashboard had lit up. Being the mechanical genius that I am, I proceeded to drive slower. I pulled into the parking lot of the college and got out to examine my truck, not taking notice of the fact that the rest of the parking lot was empty. I decided to handle my registration matters before worrying about the truck. As I walked to the business office, I wondered why there didn't seem to be any other students wandering around the campus. I reached the administration building and grasped the handle of the door, only to find the door securely locked. It suddenly hit me that of course no campus in the world would be open the day after Christmas! Feeling somewhat idiotic, I returned to my vehicle, only to find a puddle of oil forming on the pavement beneath it. I looked under the truck and discovered that an oil filter gasket had broken and the final drops of oil were trickling out. Not feeling at all pleased about how my day off was going, I trudged eight blocks to the nearest auto shop. I had to purchase a brand new filter and gasket, along with four quarts of oil. Unfortunately, I had only enough money with me to buy three of the four quarts! I was left with only some pocket change as I made my way back to the truck and tried to make the necessary repairs, soiling my clothes in the process.

By the time I arrived at the hospital, I was pleased to note that my mother's car was still in the parking lot. She was often there all day long with my father, who had just come out of his coma. Dad had recently been moved into a different room, and I was unsure of his new location. I searched every part of the hospital and still could not find my parents. I was baffled! Where could they possibly hide a stroke victim who was hardly ambulatory! Asking for directions or assistance never crossed my mind as my frustration level escalated. In disgust, I finally decided that apparently I was out of God's will in trying to have a day off! I climbed back into my truck to return in defeat to San Andreas. As I reached the freeway, one way led toward home, and the other made its way to the San Francisco Bay Area. The impulse suddenly hit me to take the city freeway and visit all of my old college friends in San Jose. Bethany Bible College was located in Santa Cruz County near San Jose. I quickly weighed my options. I had just enough gas to get to San Jose and back to San Andreas. I could stay the night with one of my friends and return to San Andreas in the morning. Even if I had to sleep on a park bench, I was determined to enjoy my day off!

There are times when I question the brain God gave me. I have done many things in my life that now serve the sole purpose of entertaining audiences when I retell the events. Many a listener has ended up in fits of laughter and disbelief, but the worrisome thing is that the stories are true! I didn't know as I drove to San Jose that I was in the midst of one such event. The wonderful thing about God is how He so often uses such moments to steer us in the direction of blessings!

I was nearing San Jose when it suddenly occurred to me that I didn't actually have any friends in San Jose. This was a most astonishing revelation as I sped toward my destination. Anyone I had known during college would of course be home with his family for Christmas, and I didn't know where any of my friends' families lived! By this time, I had reached the outskirts of San Jose. A name suddenly came to mind. Shari Hanson! We had written a few letters to each other, and I still remembered the address! I stopped at a gas station and looked in the phone book. There was a Hanson still listed at that address. I bought a city map with my remaining money and didn't even have enough change left to phone and ask whether I could stop by.

I pulled up to the house and tried to make myself look more presentable. My knock on the door was answered by an attractive young woman who resembled Shari. Thinking it might be her sister, I was about to ask her whether Shari was home when the woman recognized me and invited me inside. Shari had cut her long hair and was no longer wearing glasses. We enthusiastically chatted as I noticed all the homey sights and smells of Christmas. The house was filled with the aroma of dinner being prepared. I thought to myself that if I were to hang around a little longer, I would probably be invited for dinner. Sure enough, as dinnertime approached, Shari's mother appeared in the doorway and said, "John, I'm sure you have other plans, but you're welcome to join us for dinner tonight." I told her I thought I could fit that into my schedule, and I soon found myself enjoying a delicious meal with the Hanson family. Shari's parents were curious about what I was doing in San Jose. I found this to be a rather embarrassing question and did my best to avoid the topic. They asked about my occupation and seemed somewhat skeptical when I explained I was a pastor. My age and appearance did little to validate my claims.

After dinner, Shari invited a mutual college friend over, and we chatted for several hours. I began to wonder whether Shari's parents might offer me the guest room if I stayed around a bit longer. At nearly nine o'clock, Shari's parents announced that they had to buy some shoelaces and would be back soon. This urgent need for shoelaces seemed rather curious. Shortly thereafter, they returned and summoned me into the hallway. Shari's mom said, "Now John, I'm sure you need to be getting on your way, but we do have a spare room if you'd like to stay the night." I readily accepted their generous hospitality. Shari's dad then handed me a shoebox and said, "We thought you might need a few things, since you weren't planning to stay overnight." The box contained a razor, toothbrush, soap, deodorant and other necessities. Shari's dad then handed me a pair of neatly folded pajamas and said, "I don't know how you're accustomed to sleeping, but in my house you'll wear these." He went on to say that we were probably the same size, so I could wear some of his clothes the next day while mine were washed.

That night, after everyone was sound asleep, I dreamed I was a sick car. I was frantically trying to get the drain plug unscrewed when I awoke and found myself hunched over in bed trying to remove an imaginary drain plug from my leg! As I became more coherent I realized that I wasn't a car, I was a human—and a very ill human. I had developed a high fever and acute intestinal distress! I knew I needed to get to the bathroom urgently! I stumbled from my bed and opened the door to the hall. I could see the bathroom just steps across the hallway. I staggered desperately toward the bathroom door, dropping my drawers along the way, when suddenly, I fainted! It was one of those horrifying moments when you are unable to move and yet semiconscious of what is happening around you. There I was, flat on my face with my trousers around my knees, frantically praying, "O God! Please don't let Shari's dad come out here. He'll think I'm some kind of pervert! He'll shoot me and ask questions later!!"

God was gracious to me, and no one came to investigate. I finally struggled to my feet and into the bathroom. The next morning, however, the Hanson family had not just a transient but a sick transient on their hands! Shari's dad said, "We can't let you leave while you're sick like this. You can stay here until you get to feeling better, and then you can be on your way." I was grateful for the offer. Shari's twenty-first birthday was the next day, and I was invited to stay around for the surprise party being planned for her. I vividly remember the moment she walked into the room and everyone yelled surprise. Shari was wearing a lovely dress and looked absolutely beautiful. It was at that moment that I fell in love.

The following April, we were engaged, and on October 8, 1977, we were married. My bachelor days at the Koinonia Coffee House were over, and we moved into a small, three-room house. I continued pastoring at the San Andreas Assembly of God church for two more years.

Near San Andreas is the small, rural community of Copperopolis. The spiritual needs in this hardened town were evident. The church had been shut down long ago and the building converted into a town hall of sorts. Under the guidance of what I had come to recognize as being God's voice, I began holding services on Sunday afternoons in the rundown former church. I would preach the Sunday morning service in San Andreas and then hurriedly travel to Copperopolis. I would sweep the rustic floorboards, dust off the chairs and place a hymnal on each chair. Then I would tune up my guitar in anticipation of the congregation's arrival. But Sunday after Sunday, it was rare that anyone would come. I had visited door to door and invited the community to the services. I had handed out flyers, but no one seemed to be interested. The first time this happened, I was greatly discouraged. I wanted to simply give up and go home. Only the swallows flitting in the rafters broke the silence in this once vibrant house of worship. I began folding up the chairs and collecting the hymnals, but God's voice in me was saying, "No, you sing. You preach and do what you've come here to do."

"There's no one here," I pointed out needlessly to God. The still, small voice urged me on. "That doesn't matter. Do what I sent you here to do."

At the time, this seemed to be the single most nonsensical thing that God could ever ask me to do. Feeling utterly silly, I stepped up to the front of the room and began to sing and play the songs I had chosen for the service. I finished the songs and cleared my throat, ready to preach my message to my audience of empty chairs and curious birds. Over the months, this process repeated itself with only an occasional inquisitive spectator. Worshiping and preaching became a matter of discipline and obedience rather than something reaping obvious rewards. I remember driving home from Copperopolis, pondering this strange exercise that God seemed to be putting me through. I will never forget how He opened my heart to a whole new dimension when He explained simply, "Your unseen audience will always outnumber any audience you will ever see." I realized that every message I had spoken and every song I had sung had been cheered on by angelic participants and had made a difference in the unseen realm. Indeed, we are surrounded by a heavenly host, a cloud of witnesses.

This revelation was confirmed nearly two decades after my final visit to Copperopolis. In 1994, I was speaking at a church in San Andreas. After the service, a woman approached me and asked me to come and talk to her mother who was in the audience but unable to walk to the platform. She explained that her mother lived in a local rest home and, upon hearing that I was in town speaking, had very much wanted to meet me. I was certainly surprised and asked what had caused her interest. The daughter related to me that her parents had been pastoring in California and in their senior years had felt God specifically telling them to minister in Copperopolis. They had since planted a thriving church there. I was delighted to meet this lovely woman of God. She excitedly shook my hand and explained that from their first arrival in Copperopolis she had sensed such a sweet presence of Jesus in the town hall. She had told her husband that surely someone had spent many hours praying and preparing the way for their work. It had been years later that she came across a church bulletin in which I had written the story of my seemingly fruitless efforts in Copperopolis, and her speculations had been confirmed. They had put that bulletin on the front page of their church history, and every year on the church's anniversary, someone would read my article to the congregation and give thanks to God.

I now look with joy upon those hours I spent with the birds and the angels, learning that success has nothing to do with numbers and everything to do with obedience to God.

ELEVEN

Olive Oil Communion

IN my final year of pastoring at the church in San Andreas, I met a man named Mark Stewart during a leadership conference at Mt. Hermon, near Santa Cruz. Mark expressed his desire to start a church in the mountains, and I offered to show him around our area, Calaveras County. I drove Mark and his wife, Dottie, through Copperopolis and other nearby communities, ending up in Arnold. From San Andreas, Arnold was only forty-five minutes farther into the mountains, but it had a completely different atmosphere. Surrounded by ski slopes, lakes and golf courses, Arnold attracted vacationers, retired people and city families wanting to get away from it all. But it was a town of much need. Shari's parents were among those wanting to find a new lifestyle in the mountains and had moved to Arnold. They had become acquainted with a group of people wanting to start a church and suggested that Mark and Dottie get together with them.

I'll never forget our first meeting. Shari and I drove with Mark and Dottie to the house of one of the couples interested in forming a church, Jack and Kay Rudd. The Rudds had opened up their home for an initial gathering to plan and meet everyone face-to-face. They lived, however, at the end of a long, dirt road, which the torrential rain had turned into a difficult muddy track, at least for those unfamiliar with the route. We ended up getting stuck in the mud, and Mark and I had to get out of the car and push it down the road. Not only were we late, but we arrived soaking wet and muddy!

Our undesirable first impression didn't seem to daunt anyone, though. We soon commenced an informal weekly meeting in Arnold, rotating among private homes every Saturday night. It was clear that God was bringing together a group of people whose talents complemented one another. A team spirit and unity prevailed from the first day. We shared a vision for a new kind of fellowship, one where the ministry was overseen by a team of leaders dedicated to raising up other leaders. We were unaware that this "new" leadership structure was being adopted by fellowships all over and would one day be common. We decided that as we grew, we would break into smaller cell groups, allowing for more and more leaders to be developed. Our emphasis was on building the relationship of leaders together, working in consensus under the Holy Spirit. With much time and commitment, Mountain Christian Fellowship was finally born.

A new pastor arrived to take over the leadership of the church in San Andreas, and Shari and I moved to Arnold to join the leadership team. After about six months of meeting in private homes, we held our first Sunday morning public meeting in an old schoolhouse built in the 1850s to accommodate the huge gold-mining population. We made a point of being a very friendly church, enthusiastically embracing all who came.

Out of the initial families and individuals, God did indeed produce many influential leaders, some of whom have gone on to pastor other churches and lead other ministries. Jack and Kay Rudd were instrumental not only in the church but also in the idea to form a Christian kindergarten through twelfth-grade school. It was the first such school in the area. People at that time were very skeptical of Christian education, but with much effort and organization, Mountain Christian Academy was established in 1980. Using innovative curricula developed by Accelerated Christian Education, we were able to teach our primary and secondary level children in a close-knit family setting with the highest of academic standards. It was a tremendous joy to see our young people establish a firm foundation of faith, respect for their Creator and a hope-filled vision for the future.

Pursuing our own further education, Shari and I took a six-month leave of absence from our jobs and returned to Bethany Bible College. We had both left school before completing our bachelor's degrees. We negotiated with the college to take an unprecedented course load. The college agreed to allow me to take the thirty units I needed to graduate and Shari to take the twenty-one units she lacked. I had to attend both Bethany and a community college to obtain all the necessary classes. It was perhaps unwise to take so many units in one semester, but by the grace of God, I finished with a 4.0 grade point average, and Shari graduated summa cum laude, tied with the highest scores in her class!

In May 1983, we were presented with our long-awaited degrees. Mine had taken ten years from the time I finished high school! As a graduation present, Shari's parents treated us to a two-week vacation in Hawaii. We fell in love with the islands and decided to make them our regular vacation destination!

While at school, Shari and I had looked into the opportunities for overseas missions. We had interviewed with Overseas Missionary Fellowship and were curious about what our involvement could be. As we weighed the options, we decided it was not for us at that time. We felt God wanted us back at Mountain Christian Fellowship.

In July of 1984, I was praying one day when a vivid picture came into my mind. I saw a white ship set against a background of the South Pacific and Asia. It was a very strange experience, and I didn't know quite what to make of it. The next day was the Fourth of July, and we went to Santa Cruz to celebrate the holiday with my best friend Charlie Cohen. I described to Charlie the picture I had seen. Charlie was amazed and told me that lately he had been thinking about the same thing. He felt that God was speaking to him about ministry on a ship in the Pacific.

A few weeks later at an elders meeting one of our church leaders, Danny, suddenly said, "John, I have a scripture for you!" He then began to read the first ten verses from Isaiah 42, ending with, "Sing to the LORD a new song, his praise from the ends of the earth, you who go down to the sea, and all that is in it, you islands, and all who live in them." I had not told any of the leaders about my vision, and I was dumbfounded. Danny looked confused and said, "Oh, wait, that's not the right place. I meant to read Isaiah 45!" I have no idea what it was he read from chapter 45, because my mind was caught up in the words from chapter 42 about the sea and islands! My seaward obsession was dawning.

I had never had much to do with the sea. Charlie Cohen had been an Olympic class sailor in his youth, but I didn't know the bow from the stern. Furthermore, I really enjoyed Mountain Christian Fellowship, and I didn't want to go anywhere else. I had grown up in these beloved mountains. Besides, Shari and I wanted to have children. We had been trying without success for two years. We had every reason to stay where we were, and we did for the next six years. But all the while, the seaward thoughts were there. Just below the surface, they simmered and occasionally bubbled up. God was calling us for purposes that we couldn't possibly understand.

My interest in nautical things began to grow. I began to read all about sailing and about the South Pacific. I started watching "learn to sail" shows on TV and bought a little twelve-foot unsinkable sloop, which I tried out on a nearby lake. I soon developed a love for sailing. I became a curiosity in our church, with everyone thinking I was going through some sort of early midlife crisis! I would often talk about how a ship could be used to help people in the South Pacific to reach remote islands with the love of God. I had no idea anyone else had ever thought of this idea.

In 1985, we returned to Hawaii to celebrate my thirtieth birthday. We took a two-day excursion to the Big Island of Hawaii, staying at the Hilton in Kona. I remember looking up the hillside and seeing a large construction project with lots of activity. I decided to wander up and see what was being built. Being a kid at heart and possessing something of a construction background, I thought that maybe if I talked nicely to them they would let me operate the heavy equipment or something. I approached some workers standing next to a big pile of dirt and asked what they were making. The young man replied proudly, "This is the Plaza of Nations."

"Oh," I said. "What's it for?"

"This is a university campus. It's part of Youth With A Mission. Have you ever heard of us?" he asked.

"No," I replied.

The young man went on to describe YWAM and its international ministries and then invited me to see a video describing the mission further. I accepted the invitation and went inside to a visitor's center, where I watched a video that gave the name of this missionary campus, "Pacific and Asia Christian University." Something sparked in my mind, and I immediately remembered my vision the previous year featuring the Pacific and Asian regions. I made my way back to the hotel, noting the amusingly ambitious, underfunded project these people were undertaking.

Shari and I returned to Arnold. That August our lives were forever changed by the joy-filled arrival of our newborn son Johnny. Becoming parents was wonderful. I can still remember the feeling of bringing our little boy home from the hospital!

It was a busy time for us with our growing family and fellowship. The Lord provided a property for the church. Years earlier while I was still pastoring in San Andreas, Charlie Cohen and I would often drive up to Arnold to have lunch at the Jolly Farmer Restaurant. We would sit on the large open-air decks and gaze at the surrounding woods. I remember commenting that this would make a great place for a church. Years later, the property came up for sale, and by then, we were looking for a permanent location for our fellowship. This was prime commercial property, though, located right on the highway, and the price was prohibitive. Soon, the property was occupied by several businesses. Over time, most of them failed or moved, leaving the property virtually vacant once more and the price substantially lower. This time, our fellowship was able to purchase it and begin converting the commercial complex into a church and school facility.

As if the building project weren't enough to undertake, I decided to study Hebrew at the Fuller Seminary extension campus in San Francisco. Once I got into the seminary environment, I began taking more and more classes. I commuted the six hours to the Bay Area and back two times a week, often arriving home at one o'clock in the morning. After five such years, I had completed my master's degree.

I thoroughly enjoyed pastoring the family at Mountain Christian Fellowship. We maintained a fun church environment with much good humor. One Sunday, our youth minister, Russ, was scheduled to oversee the communion service. I arrived at the church and realized that I was supposed to conduct a baby dedication in the morning's service as well, but I had forgotten and had left my vial of anointing oil at home. I found some olive oil in the kitchen and used it to fill a small communion cup, which I placed on the shelf of the pulpit. At the beginning of the service, I performed the baby dedication, replacing the remaining oil back under the pulpit. Later, Russ approached the podium and the communion service began. The communion elements were distributed, and Russ shared a moving message. In our fellowship, we had agreed upon using white grape juice in place of wine for the sake of the new, light-colored carpets. Russ had set his cup on the pulpit shelf, oblivious to the fact that my olive oil was already there. As he prayed over the drink, I noticed that he accidentally grabbed the wrong cup! My inward debate over whether I should speak up and ruin the moment or remain quiet and try not to smile too much was cut short by Russ's solemnly downing the entire cup of "juice." Russ grimaced as he hastily concluded and rushed to the bathroom, and I had the pleasure of explaining to a surprised but amused congregation what had just happened!

As much as I loved my church and home in the mountains, my seaward obsessions were ever present. Something in me was hearing the call of God to far-off places. Something in me would never be content until I acted upon that call.

TWELVE

"Pastor, Don't Shoot!"

LITTLE did I know that the joys of pastoring and the expectation of our Pacific calling were about to be placed into the crucible of the greatest personal and emotional pain of my life. I was about to undergo a series of personal and professional stresses that would strip me of my dreams, beliefs and courage.

Our church was experiencing an exciting time of growth. We had just purchased the old Jolly Farmer Restaurant and had undertaken the monumental task of remodeling the facilities for the use of our church and school. Under the best of circumstances, property purchases and building projects often place significant pressure on churches and their leadership. For me, this project's stress was compounded by the fact that the general contractor who had taken charge of the renovations was unable to continue the job. Since I had experience as a builder, I was left to assume his role. In addition, our very gifted worship leader and his family answered a call to pastor in San Jose. My passable musical talent, combined with budget restraints, made it necessary for me to take on his duties as well.

Although I have always been able to tend to a great diversity of tasks, my already full plate of commitments proved to be too much. I was juggling too many mental balls, and losing my grip was imminent. I regularly feared that some real estate contingency, permit legality, congregational or personal detail was being overlooked and unattended. I couldn't sleep. My wife was advising me to ask the other elders for help, but I was reluctant to impose on an already overtaxed leadership. I did not want to disappoint everyone by dropping the ball. I never dreamed that soon I would be left with no alternative.

Our lives were further complicated by two very delicate situations. A worker with Child Protective Services had elicited my help with a very religious and distressed family. The troubled parents had become paranoid that the state would infringe upon their religious life and had therefore withdrawn their ten children from school. The family was living in squalor in a twenty-six-foot trailer home without electricity or plumbing.

I went to the home and, after cleaning out their bathtub, which had been turned into an indoor cesspool, made arrangements for the children to stay with some families in our church. The children responded well to these caring homes, but the parents soon came to despise our involvement. After school one day, in the midst of personal and legal battles, the parents commandeered most of their children and disappeared to parts unknown. The oldest daughter, who stayed with us, successfully resisted their efforts, remaining to graduate with honors and a full scholarship to a California university.

In the middle of that unpleasant situation, I also became involved in the perilous efforts of a local family to remove their young grandson from a gang-operated crack house. When police officers eventually removed the child, death threats and bona fide death contracts ensued. The new legal guardians were forced to live incognito to avoid risk to their lives or kidnaping of the child for two months until a formal custody hearing could be completed. I was one of the few who knew the couple's whereabouts. I had also agreed to testify in court as to my knowledge of the situation. Immediately, my own family and I became the subject of threats and intimidation. Messages were sent, phone calls were received and cars would pass by slowly as someone leaned out the window pretending to point and pull the trigger of a gun. The gang's tactics were effective. We were frightened. I was shaken to the point of finding a small .22 caliber handgun my dad had given me and keeping it near my bed for protection.

The situation came to a head one night as we were sleeping in our secluded mountain home. I was abruptly awakened by the sound of someone diligently rattling each door and window latch attempting to gain entry. As I quietly rose from bed and pulled on my robe and slippers, Shari was startled awake by the sound of large rocks being thrown onto the roof. She was petrified by the thought that the recent threats made on our family were coming to pass.

"I'll get Johnny," she said as I slipped the gun out of the drawer beside the bed and located the ammunition. I walked quietly to the front door, my heart pounding. I opened the door and marched defiantly down the long driveway, straining to see in the darkness. I heard movement in the trees and several people running. I spun toward the noise and fired twice into the air. A fleeing shadow uttered a profanity and ducked behind a nearby bush. With little caution, I approached the stooped silhouette, wondering whether I should shoot.

"Who are you!" I demanded.

A familiar and intimidated voice trembled, "Don't shoot me, Pastor. I'm Eric, from the youth group—I'm really sorry we tried to TP your house!" He quickly explained that he and other members of the youth group had playfully and covertly decided to play a practical joke on us by wrapping our house and trees in toilet paper.

My relief was exceeded only by my embarrassment as I contemplated the repercussions in our small community when the story got out about the trigger-happy pastor who threatens his youth at gunpoint! I called out to the others and asked them to join me in the open field by the lake in front of our house. We made a solemn vow that I would not tell their parents that they had been out that night if they didn't tell anyone that I had tried to gun them down! They explained that one of them had gotten the idea of trying to scare us by rattling the doors and windows and throwing rocks onto the roof. They had no idea, of course, of the fearful ordeal our family had been facing or how close we all came that night to an unthinkable tragedy.

As a typically intense Christmas holiday season came and went, my exterior was beginning to resemble my beleaguered interior. I arrived one Saturday morning to supervise the workday activities. Immediately several volunteers came to seek direction and decisions. I was struck with a profound disability to think clearly or offer any advice. Perplexed by my condition, I hurriedly asked for a list of needed materials and left in my truck for the building supply store. From the moment I left the church, I began to cry uncontrollably. Unable to compose myself, I returned to the church and asked one of the elders to pray for me. I explained between sobs that I did not know why I was crying or how to stop. The elder prayed and then replied, "We have to get you out of here!"

Taking me home, the elder issued orders for an immediate vacation. I complied without protest, and after two weeks, I returned to find the church had risen to the occasion. A friend was leading the music, and the remodeling was progressing nicely. Over the next few months, I resumed my roles, but my emotional condition was delicate. Some days and weeks were decidedly worse than others. It was obvious that my normally positive, unsinkable personality had become irritable and depressive. I had to struggle to maintain any semblance of an amicable attitude toward my work and my colleagues. I was becoming cynical and mistrusting, doubting the competence of those around me. My wife often bore the brunt of my disappointment and anger. Spiritual disciplines became frustrating and ineffectual as their frequency dwindled. Every time I felt myself rebounding, something always knocked me back. I found myself blaming God. I felt like I was losing my mind, my life and my faith all at the same time.

Perhaps somewhere in the recesses of my darkened mind, a glimmer of hope refused to be extinguished, but for now it was all I could do to get out of bed each day. Any plans or vision I had once optimistically entertained had long since been engulfed in the sea of gloom that occupied my every thought. I existed and grappled with the terrifying question of what had become of me. I was in an ever-downward spiral, and it would be some time before I was able to even consider how to reverse my descent.

The church leaders were extremely supportive and gave me plenty of time off, always ready with words of encouragement and reassurance. I began reading books like *Burnout* by Myron Rush and *Wounded Warriors* by Loren Sanford. Through caring friends like Foursquare pastors Al Soto and Jim Hayford, I learned how widespread this problem was and that I was not alone. There were many people suffering as I was, in and out of the church, whom I could now relate to and perhaps could one day help.

It was during this time that I learned much about my own limits and about leadership and delegation. I learned about patience and love from my family and the church leaders who protected me and offered solace. Most important, I began to understand the unconditional love of my Father in heaven. For the first time in months, my heart began to rejoice as I recognized His love that had persisted even when my mind was dark and my faith was dead. I realized that He loves me even though my thoughts and deeds are ambiguous and self-seeking. I learned that my relationship with God never had anything to do with me but that it was all His doing. God made it clear that I did not choose Him; He had chosen me. God revealed His faithfulness, His reality in my life. In my heart I knew that truth, that reality, would set me free. It was the intensity and depth of God's pure, unbounded love that finally began to liberate my mind from the numbing fog. My recovery was not immediate, but it had begun, and I had no doubt that I was not alone on my journey, no matter how long it might take.

My good friend Jack Rudd stopped by one day to chat. When he asked me how I was doing, I replied that I was doing great! It had been quite some time since my burnout episode, and the unpleasant memories had now become an impetus to reach out to others undergoing similar difficulties. I felt capable of facing life without undue anxiety, and my personality had returned to its previous somewhat "normal" state. I was back into the swing of things, exercising more wisdom and putting into practice what I had learned, not eager to ever repeat my lessons. I was happy and content with my personal life. Shari had given birth to our second child, a beautiful little girl we named Angela Eden, meaning delightful messenger. Johnny was nearly four and was growing up fast. I told Jack I was loving life in Arnold and hoped to live there for the rest of my life.

Over breakfast a few days later, Shari and I began talking about our future goals and dreams. For some time, I had not even considered the

Pacific vision I had once cherished. It had seemingly been one of the casualties of my previous personal battle. Of late, though, I had caught myself thinking about the calling I had sensed in the past. I wondered whether this was God rebirthing the vision in me. As we conversed, Shari mentioned that she had been experiencing the same rebirth of vision and wondered whether it might be time for us to heed this call of God. After much discussion, we both agreed it was time to leave our beloved home and resign the pastorate at Mountain Christian Fellowship. We believed we were to step out in faith and trust God for our finances. This was no small step for our growing family. Furthermore, we concluded the place to start was Kona, Hawaii, on the hillside university campus that we had seen under construction years earlier.

The only thing we knew about Youth With A Mission was what I had seen on the video that day in Hawaii. We began to correspond with the YWAM campus and learned about a branch of the ministry called Mission Builders. It seemed that construction was still going on at the campus and workers were needed. Room and board were provided for those willing to work and provide their own way to Kona. This seemed like an easy first step. It was in Hawaii, a place we knew and loved. It was not a foreign country. It was a practical job I knew I could do. And it didn't require a lengthy commitment. We would also have a chance to assess the ministry and the other opportunities available. Although the campus had recently changed its name to University of the Nations, it maintained its focus on the Pacific and Asian regions, which seemed to be where God was directing us.

In due time, I presented our plans to the leadership team at Mountain Christian Fellowship. Reluctantly but unanimously, the leaders began to see that this was the direction we needed to take. My brother Bart had been the principal of our Christian school for four years and had served as an associate pastor. The leadership team asked Bart to take over for me in the senior pastoral position. Shari and I began sending out letters and forming our personal network of supporters. Our desire to move on to the next step was growing quickly, but ending our pastorate was the hardest professional decision I had ever made. Leaving our friends, a regular salary and our longstanding home was torturous. At our final service at Mountain Christian Fellowship, Shari and I arranged to serve communion personally to every member of the congregation. It was a very special time as we said our farewells.

We packed the final items and prepared for our flight to Kona in November 1990. Shari wasn't feeling well and remarked that if she didn't know better she would think she was pregnant. She was! And so with one unexpected passenger, our growing family loaded onto the plane bound for the unknown.

As we jetted through the sky, leaving behind our familiar home, I thought of our Pacific island destination. Was this the fulfillment of the vision I had seen? Just before leaving California, I had addressed a Messianic Jewish congregation in the San Francisco Bay Area. The congregation has a regular cycle of readings from the prophets and had asked me to read at its Shabbat service. I was given the text, only to find myself reading from Isaiah 42, the same verses that had been read to me years earlier!

> Sing to the LORD a new song, his praise from the ends of the earth, you who go down to the sea, and all that is in it, you islands, and all who live in them....Let them give glory to the LORD and proclaim his praise in the islands. (Isaiah 42:10,12)

THIRTEEN

"You Who Go Down to the Sea"

W E landed in Kona and were loaded with our abundant luggage into a van to take us to our new residence. After dropping off our bags, we were taken to the worship service already in progress under the open-air pavilion at the center of the University of the Nations campus. As we approached, we could hear the worship leader singing his brand-new song, which would later be recorded by Integrity Music. Although I had never before heard the song, I recognized the words immediately. "Sing to the Lord a new song, sing His praise to the ends of the earth / you who go down to the sea, you who live in the islands, if you live in the city, lift your voice and sing out / Glory, glory Lord, we give you glory Lord..."[1] This song, based on the words of Isaiah 42, became an immediate favorite.

The university campus consisted of several old hotel buildings along with a few new buildings that had been constructed on the property. The Plaza of Nations that I had seen being built years before was now a beautiful fountain surrounded by flagpoles displaying the flags of many different nations of the world. It seemed this was one of many hundreds of locations that YWAM operated all over the world. In fact, YWAM's founder, Loren Cunningham, had personally visited nearly every nation on earth, and YWAM teams had worked in every nation except one—Pitcairn Island in the South Pacific.

Shari and I had been accepted to attend the three-month training school offered at this campus. Called Crossroads Discipleship Training School, or CDTS, the school was specially designed to accommodate families and, among other things, provide an introduction to the YWAM missions environment. The school was due to start in April 1991. For the five months until the school was to open, I would be working as a mission builder.

I soon discovered that my assigned carpentry job consisted of working long hours roofing in the hot Kona sun, so when an opening came in the electrical department, I happily volunteered! The man in charge of the electrical department, Bill Goulding, was suffering from Parkinson's disease and had decided to retire. I was privileged as this genial man, once a senior engineer for Chevrolet manufacturing, took me under his wing and allowed me to glean from his years of experience and vast expertise. Just before leaving, Bill asked me to finish a project he had started. He had promised to do the electrical work on a new addition to the Cunninghams' home but had not had a chance to finish. I was happy to help my new friend fulfill his promise and was blessed with the opportunity to get to know the Cunninghams. During that time, Loren happened to be at home recovering from health problems, which provided me with the unique opportunity to spend time with one of the busiest men I have ever met.

In December, a video was presented at a Friday night meeting that showed a new ship that had just been given to YWAM by a New Zealand businessman named Sid Lane. The ship, called the *Pacific Ruby*, would be home ported in Tauranga, New Zealand, and used for missions work in the South Pacific islands! Shari and I were astounded. This was so similar to our vision! Eager to learn more, I contacted the office for Mercy Ships in New Zealand. It seemed that this was the third ship to join the branch of YWAM known as Mercy Ships. These ships were dedicated to the "two-handed" approach to the gospel, meeting both physical and spiritual needs by taking medical, dental, construction and evangelism teams to developing world ports around the globe. This newest and smallest addition to the fleet would be operating primarily in the South Pacific.

The CDTS that Shari and I were to attend would finish at the end of June. Typically, students then participate in a two-month outreach to various destinations, although in a Crossroads school, this outreach phase is optional. Shari would not be able to go on outreach, as our baby was due mid-June, but she was supportive in my desire to see whether anything was available in July and August with the *Pacific Ruby*.

The Mercy Ships office responded that there was indeed an outreach planned for July and August but that it was a special outreach and Loren Cunningham would be personally handpicking the team members. Even though I did not know the special outreach destination, I wrote to Loren, describing my vision from years earlier and my desire to work in the islands with a ship ministry. A few days later, I went to the Cunninghams' house to continue the electrical installation. Around noon, Loren invited me to take a break. Over lunch he began to speak about the upcoming *Pacific Ruby* outreach. He explained how there was one remaining country that YWAM had not yet visited. Previous attempts to organize an outreach to this nation had all failed for one reason or another. This final country, tiny Pitcairn Island, was the smallest protectorate of the British Commonwealth, with a population of only fifty-eight on a two-square-mile rock situated in the middle of the Pacific. The isolated island, located halfway between Australia and South America, had no airstrip and no conducive anchorage for boats, making it a very difficult travel destination.

Loren was excited as he explained that YWAM had finally received permission from the Pitcairn government and the British High Commissioner to visit Pitcairn and that the new Mercy Ship would be providing the transport. Loren would be choosing a small team composed of his family and medical and dental personnel to sail with the *Ruby*'s crew to Pitcairn in fulfillment of his own personal vision to reach every nation with the gospel of Jesus Christ. "Pitcairn stands as a final goal to complete our obedience to the Lord," he said earnestly.

"The bottom line is to obey God in His commandment to go into every country to share the good news of Jesus—no matter how small the country or what it takes to get there."

Certainly, Jesus must have been thinking of remote Pitcairn when he said, "You will be My witnesses in Jerusalem, and in all Judea and Samaria, and to the ends of the earth." One of the Mercy Ships' staff members even calculated that Pitcairn is literally the opposite side of the earth from the Holy Land, giving this scripture in the first chapter of Acts new meaning.

I recognized the significance of this special outreach for this man who over thirty years before had seen a vision of waves of young people washing over every continent, every shore of the globe. His vision had given birth to what was now the world's largest interdenominational missions organization. I felt honored to be sharing lunch with this man as he personally explained the outreach to me and a bit embarrassed for having suggested that I be included on the landmark team. As I expressed that thought to him, he surprised me by saying, "Oh, no, John. I've read your letter and prayed about your vision, and I believe you are to come with us. You have carpentry, plumbing and electrical skills as well as pastoral expertise. I have recommended you to David and Linda Cowie, the directors of the *Pacific Ruby* ministry."

I remember leaving Loren's company feeling stunned! I couldn't wait to tell Shari. Our CDTS hadn't even started yet, and my outreach was already arranged. And what an outreach it was! I was amazed at how God was interweaving the fulfillment of so many visions.

April arrived, and the training began. Shari, in her very pregnant state, was suffering quite a bit from the Hawaiian heat. We were excited to begin the school and meet an influx of new people onto the campus who would become close friends as we went through the three-month training course together. Even though this was one of the smallest Crossroads classes the campus had had in some time, among the thirty students were many couples near our age. I remember meeting Randy and Janet Gradishar. Not being a sports fan, I failed to recognize this former Denver Bronco seven-year all-pro football star. It was not until someone later told me who he was that I learned of my new friend's celebrity status! Other couples like John and Cherie Day from Canada and Bruce and Jane Patten from Australia soon became our good friends. And then there was John Lindeman. John's wife, Stephanie, had already completed a CDTS and had strongly encouraged John to take a break from his high-powered business job in New Zealand to attend this school. I found John to be a fascinating businessman as well as an unashamedly genuine and open human being.

With the support and assistance of these new friends, we made it through the struggles of the coming three months. Shari began to experience problems with her pregnancy. An ultrasound at the doctor's office revealed that the baby had stopped growing, a serious condition known as intrauterine growth retardation. The doctor recommended that Shari remain in bed and refrain from all activity for several days until she could be flown to the larger hospital in Honolulu where more sophisticated equipment could be used to assess her condition. Our fellow students rallied behind us in prayer as we anxiously awaited the Honolulu trip. Three days later, we flew to Honolulu. The doctor there was amazed to see the results from her test, as it seemed that our little baby had miraculously grown the equivalent of three normal weeks in three days' time! We rejoiced as we flew back to Kona to witness to God's power and answered prayers. On June 20, 1991, as the training neared completion, Shari gave birth to our second daughter, little Lauren Alana, a Hawaiian name meaning gift or offering.

Our new Crossroads friends came through for us again as the time came to raise the necessary finances for my outreach. Several of them presented me with checks and best wishes as I prepared for the historic sail to Pitcairn.

On July 6, our whole family bustled into the Kona airport. Although I was thrilled to be heading to Rarotonga to join the *Pacific Ruby*, I was torn as I helped my intrepid wife, new babe in her arms and our other two young children at her side, load onto their direct flight home to California. Shari and I were embarking on our longest time of separation since we had been married. I would not see my family again for the next fifty-two days. I was about to gain a new appreciation for mariners who spend so many months at sea away from their families. But I knew my suffering would be nothing compared to the hardships that Shari would be tackling on her own. With three kids, she would be having the real outreach! I was pleased that she would have the support of our families back home in Arnold.

After loading Shari and the children with all of their paraphernalia onto their flight, I literally had to run back down the concourse to where my flight had already given its final boarding call. I clambered onto the plane and took my seat beside the window. Looking out I could see the plane holding my family—my world. I prayed for their safety and for my own.

About an hour after Shari and our kids landed in San Francisco, my plane touched down in Rarotonga, the largest of the Cook Islands. A couple from Rarotonga whom I had met in Kona picked me up at the airport. They had invited me to stay with them for a few nights before I moved on board the ship. The *Ruby* had already arrived into port, and I was eager to see the ship for the first time and to deliver the mail for the crew that had been sent with me from their friends and former crew members in Kona. I would soon find out for myself just how out of touch one can feel while on board a ship in the middle of the Pacific Ocean. The crew had become adept at employing creative and sometimes elaborate methods to receive letters and news from the rest of the world. I happened to be one of this port's more convenient systems!

Arriving at the dock, I immediately spotted the *Pacific Ruby* with the familiar YWAM logo of a person running across the globe carrying a torch. I gazed for several moments at the 140-foot white ship, with its blue and green logo painted on the smokestack, set against the stunning background of this South Pacific island paradise. In amazement, it struck me that it had been seven years ago, nearly to the day, that I had seen my vision of a white ship in the Pacific and Asia. God truly has remarkable ways of working out the details!

FOURTEEN

Pitcairn Island

W I T H the mail delivery tucked securely under my arm, I gingerly stepped onto the narrow plank connecting the gently bobbing ship to the concrete wharf. As I jumped onto the deck of the ship, I found myself ducking to keep from hitting my head on the steel beams of the upper deck above me. This ship would definitely take some getting used to. Everything seemed to be a few sizes smaller to accommodate the maximum number of people and equipment in the least possible space. I was led to a heavy wooden door that opened to reveal a narrow passage with stairs going up and down. The stairs could more accurately be described as glorified ladders, each step able to accommodate about one half of my actual foot length! If I thought the stairs were difficult to maneuver now, wait till the ship started sailing.

Making my way carefully down into the interior of the ship, I was pleased to enter a much larger, spacious room with couches around its perimeter. The ceiling was still too low for me to stand up straight, and unbeknownst to me, this was the largest room on the ship. I had wandered into the main lounge, where a crew meeting was in progress. The first mate's wife, Princess, was pregnant and feeling too ill to continue with the sail and would therefore be returning shortly to New Zealand. The love for this gentle woman was evident as the crew members prayed earnestly for her health and the health of her unborn baby. Thinking of our recent experience with Lauren Alana, I spoke up with a prayer for Princess. More than one pair of curious eyes looked to see who this unknown voice belonged to and what this person was doing on their ship. I was introduced as the first of Loren's team to arrive. Without hesitation, the crew welcomed me with open arms. Then I realized they had all spotted the bundle of mail I was carrying!

After the meeting, Princess's husband, Jesse, introduced himself and showed me to the lower deck cabin that he and I would be sharing for the rest of the sail. I felt immediately at home on this little ship, even though I knew I would be facing many adjustments in lifestyle. I could sense the openness and family atmosphere in this unique little community, and I was pleased to be a part of it.

Over the coming days in Rarotonga, I received my initiation into island culture. I was taught how to eat an orange, Rarotongan style. First you bite a piece of the peel off and suck out all the juice. Then you turn the entire orange inside out to eat the pulp. I observed the island men wearing their brightly colored lava-lavas, knee-length wraparound skirts that tied on the side. For formal occasions, the men would wear slightly longer gray or dark blue lava-lavas made of a heavier material. It was amazing to watch the ease with which they could modestly sit on the floor in their customary cross-legged positions. I had a feeling it would be some time before I would feel comfortable attempting this particular island custom!

I could understand the benefits of wearing the lightweight, loose-fitting lava-lavas. The temperatures were far above what I had almost gotten used to in Kona! The small, stuffy cabin Jesse and I were sharing became too hot for us one night, and we decided to sleep on the floor of the air-conditioned bridge. As we slept, the weather began to deteriorate, sending dangerous swells into the harbor. Jesse was awakened by someone calling his name. Thinking I must have mumbled in my slumber, he fell back asleep. But after two more awakenings to someone calling his name, Jesse recalled the biblical story of Samuel and Eli and rose to inspect the ship. On his rounds, he discovered that one of the lines holding us to the wharf had broken under the strain of the heavy swells. He quickly got help and resecured the ship, thanking God for his repeated wake-up call. I slept through the entire episode.

After a month-long evangelism outreach, we prepared for our departure from Rarotonga. Our next destination was Papeete, Tahiti, the "Paris of the Pacific." In addition to refueling and reprovisioning in this lively French Polynesian port, we would be joined by more members of Loren's team, including dentist Charlie Roberts and his assistant Donna Livingston. Then it was a several-day sail to the Gambier Islands to pick up Loren and his family. The Gambiers are the easternmost of the long chain of islands of French Polynesia and are the last dot of soil to which airplanes fly. Some three hundred miles to the southeast we would find Pitcairn, but first we had to maneuver through the coral reefs of Mangareva, Gambier's largest isle. We approached Mangareva with considerable caution, already two days behind schedule because of strong headwinds. The water was crystal clear, revealing the dangerous coral heads getting closer and closer to our fragile hull.

At last the captain called the ship to a halt a mile or two out from the island, indicating that to move in closer would be too threatening to the ship. In the failing light, the inflatable landing craft was put overboard, and its crew went off in search of Loren and his team. Finally, in the inky blackness, lights began to move toward us. It was a joyful reunion as the launch arrived with Loren and his party, full of anticipation for the voyage ahead. We excitedly welcomed the Cunninghams on board. I was honored to lead a time of singing and worship in the *Ruby*'s main lounge as we immediately weighed anchor to complete our historic passage to Pitcairn.

The general atmosphere of excitement and joy soon subsided as the *Ruby* resumed her customary rolling and pitching. People began retreating to the comfort of their bunks, ill and drowsy from the various anti-seasick remedies. Loren soon withdrew to his cabin and, like many others, was rarely seen over the remainder of the voyage. I spent many hours with his dear wife, Darlene, sitting on a bench out on deck, chatting and whiling away the hours as we crossed the mighty Pacific.

Over the course of our 1,175-nautical-mile voyage from Tahiti to Pitcairn, I volunteered for deck duty, standing four-hour watches on the bridge of the ship. I met our captain, Tony, a native of the Cook Islands in his late seventies. Captain Tony had been a sailor for most of his years and knew these waters like the back of his hand. His quiet, confident, soft-spoken manner was enough to calm our anxieties even as we hit rough seas.

One night I was trying to sleep in my bunk, but the violent motion of the ship was tossing me back and forth like a child's small toy. The sound of the waves crashing into the hull began to alarm me as I wondered whether the tiny vessel could withstand the pounding. I cautiously climbed out of my bunk, timing each move with the rolls of the ship. Holding on for dear life, I made my way up the stairs to the bridge, where I found Captain Tony standing quietly in the darkened room, watching serenely out the front windows. I made my way over to his side, bracing myself on the walls and standing with my legs as wide apart as possible to keep my balance.

"Wow, it's kind of heavy weather we've got going right now!" I remarked, expecting he would say, "Oh yeah, we've really got a rough one tonight."

Instead he coolly replied, "It's pretty normal for the Pacific, really." That was when I knew I was in trouble!

Also on board the *Ruby* for the outreach to Pitcairn was Professor Herbert Ford, director of the Pitcairn Islands Study Center at Pacific Union College in California and one of the leading experts on the history of Pitcairn Island. Having spent much of his life researching the intriguing past of Pitcairn's inhabitants, Professor Ford's lifelong dream to go to Pitcairn was being fulfilled on this voyage. The professor prepared us for our arrival and kept us occupied for hours with his stories about Pitcairn as we "stood" watch, often in the prone position, on the bridge of the ship.

Pitcairn Island is home to the descendants of the mutineers from the infamous British ship HMS *Bounty*. The *Bounty*, under the strict command of Captain William Bligh, was in the South Pacific on Royal Command, procuring breadfruit trees for transport to the British West Indies. Having fallen in love with the women and lifestyle in Tahiti, many crew members did not want to complete their mission and leave the South Pacific. On April 28, 1789, en route to the West Indies, a number of the crew, led by the master's mate, Fletcher Christian, mutinied against Captain Bligh. Bligh and eighteen loyal officers were set adrift with sparse provisions in a twenty-three-foot boat with six oars and a small sail. With no chart to establish his position or the location of hospitable land, Bligh proved his excellent seamanship by successfully navigating his tiny boat and crew over thirty-six hundred miles, arriving at Timor, Java, almost two months later.

The mutineers returned to Tahiti to pick up their female companions. Loading the *Bounty* with fresh provisions and ample livestock, the mutineers, along with nine women and eighteen Tahitian men and boys, set sail in search of a refuge where the British Admiralty would never find them. After several unsuccessful attempts to settle on various islands, ten remaining mutineers, twelve women and six Tahitian men sailed the *Bounty* to the remote, isolated and uninhabited island of Pitcairn. The formidable, near-vertical cliffs provided no harbor or easy access to the island. After exploring the island's perimeter, Christian finally selected a small indentation and ran the ship onto the rocks. In this less-than-sheltered harbor, later named Bounty Bay, the men dropped anchor and tethered the ship to a sturdy tree ashore. On January 23, a date still celebrated on Pitcairn Island, after stripping the *Bounty* of every usable item, what remained of the ship was destroyed by fire. Left with no means of escape, this unusual company founded a colony that remained undiscovered until 1808, nearly twenty years after the mutiny.

Fletcher Christian took charge of the new community, but after several years, chaos broke out among its few inhabitants, eventually ending in the murders or tragic deaths of all but one of the mutineers and ten of the women. Fortunately, by that time, twenty-three children had been added to the population, including Fletcher's first son, Thursday October Christian. The final mutineer, Alexander Smith, changed his name to John Adams and became the revered patriarch of Pitcairn's society, learning to read one of the few books on the island— the Bible. He became a devout believer and led the island's entire population in converting to Christianity. Years later, long after the first passing vessel had been amazed to find English-speaking people claiming to be British on the remote island, Seventh-Day Adventist missionaries came to Pitcairn. The society soon adopted the Seventh-Day Adventist faith.

The Pitcairn community grew and flourished as one of the most extraordinary cultural experiments of all time. Over the years, Pitcairn's population outgrew its small island home. In March 1831, the entire population of 87 was moved to Tahiti. Disease and amoral conduct quickly convinced the Pitcairners that they were better off on Pitcairn, and so by September of the same year, they were returned to their island. Again in the late 1850s, Pitcairn's entire population decided to desert the island. This time all 194 inhabitants boarded a ship bound for Norfolk Island, a recently abandoned British penal colony just north of New Zealand. Although it was a bigger island, many Pitcairners longed for home, and in 1859 and again in 1864, several families returned to Pitcairn. Since then, Pitcairners have continued to inhabit both islands.

Aboard the *Pacific Ruby*, six Pitcairners were being transported home. To get from Pitcairn to Norfolk or New Zealand and back again, Pitcairners have learned the art of catching a ride with any passing ship. We would also be taking two Pitcairners back to New Zealand with us. I was fascinated by the lore of Pitcairn's history, but like Loren Cunningham, I believed that God had a significant plan for Pitcairn's future. Pitcairn's society is a poignant example to the rest of the world. Pitcairners pay no taxes, but the men gather once a week to work on community projects. Their strong sense of community and devotion to God's principles have kept their island free of crime and the abuses that plague most societies. The door to the old jail on Pitcairn rusted open long ago.

After eight endless days at sea, we could see the morning sun revealing the outline of a sheer-cliffed rock off the *Ruby*'s bow. There is no barrier reef surrounding Pitcairn, just the sudden rock walls jutting out of the ocean, rising up to 1,138 feet above the water. The night before, we had come into radio range with the island and had been greeted by Tom Christian, the great-great-great grandson of Fletcher Christian. Shortwave radio is Pitcairn's main link to the outside world.

We invited the island residents to come out to the *Ruby* for breakfast in the morning.

In the day's first light we spied the island's longboat bouncing over the waves toward the ship, carrying forty of the island's fifty-eight residents. Every member of the *Ruby*'s entourage waited eagerly to welcome the Pitcairners aboard. As they neared, we could hear their voices blended in sweet harmony, singing hymns of welcome. Pulling their boat alongside the *Ruby*, they were helped onto the ship, bringing with them handcrafted items and Pitcairn hats and t-shirts. Pitcairn's income is largely derived from the sale of handicrafts and souvenirs to passing vessels. Everyone traveling near Pitcairn wants a memento from this remote locale.

After a hearty breakfast, thirty YWAM team members clambered with the Pitcairners onto the longboat and motored expertly to the short concrete jetty protruding into Bounty Bay. To the sound of cheers from the entire team on board, Loren was the first to set foot on Pitcairn. With a broad grin, he began shaking the hands of the island residents who had come to welcome us ashore. Those of us who were not up to the challenge of climbing their steep, thirty-degree "Hill of Difficulty" were shuttled on all-terrain vehicles, the islanders' only means of transport other than their feet. Reaching the top, we observed Western-style wooden buildings reminiscent of America's pioneer days. With building supplies at a minimum, most homes and structures are made from mismatched pieces of timber dropped by passing ships, some painted and some not, with corrugated iron roofing. Of Pitcairn's twelve hundred acres, less than one third are cultivated. The rest consists of mainly mountainous, rocky cliffs and heavily wooded areas too steep for the growing of crops. There is a plentiful supply of breadfruit, plantains, yams, taro root and paper mulberry for the making of tapa cloth, while the waters surrounding the island abound with mackerel, rock cod, red snapper, crayfish and tuna.

Passing through the island's only village, Adamstown, we observed the church, public square and courthouse together with the post office, library and dispensary—the latter three all in the same building. I sat on a bench in the little town square near the bell that is rung to announce church services, public workdays and the arrival of ships. I was joined by a friendly older woman descended from Fletcher Christian's line. The woman took great pleasure in telling me about her island home and pointing out the tall Norfolk pine her grandfather had planted. She told me of the island's history and the *Bounty* mutineers and asked whether I had been to see their cemetery yet. She said, "You must go there. It's just down the road, and people are dying to get in there!" My new friend laughed with delight at her own joke as I realized that she had done a splendid job of setting me up! I suppose it is not often they get to try out their jokes on new people. I wandered over to the post office and bought postcards and Pitcairn stamps and had them canceled with the day's date. Postage stamps are another lucrative source of income for Pitcairn's economy.

In contrast to the normal lifestyle on Pitcairn, our arrival brought a flurry of activity as the medical teams brought equipment ashore and set up their clinics. Dr. Bill and Bobbie Johnson, a surgeon and a nurse from California, restocked the island's dispensary with thousands of dollars worth of donated supplies and then set up shop to see patients. They performed several surgeries, including a complicated hernia repair.

The optometry team began seeing patients and distributing glasses, while the dental "drill 'em and fill 'em" team examined nearly every mouth on the island. Island residents usually suffer with tooth pain until they need an extraction. A local heavy equipment operator doubles as their part-time dentist. During our brief stay, the *Ruby*'s dental team filled 115 cavities, finding 17 in one mouth!

One of the ship's engineers began a two-day project to repair a valuable boat motor. The residents were grateful, as normally such things take over six months to be shipped out for repairs.

That night, members of the ship's teams were hosted in the rustic and rambling homes of various Pitcairn families. Although lacking indoor plumbing and other comforts, many homes had a TV and VCR, along with a number of videotapes, since there is no television reception available. The island generators function for only a few hours each evening, providing power to all the homes on Pitcairn. My hostess cooked delicious meals over the open fire on her kitchen floor, although some Pitcairn kitchens were equipped with modern appliances. As with every home, just outside was a large garden and fruit trees supplying year-round vegetables, bananas, oranges, mangos, papayas and the sweetest of grapefruit. Rainwater is collected in large tanks and used for drinking, although in the dry season there are intermittent springs in the valley west of Adamstown.

My hostess, an elderly, energetic woman, served me a bowl of rice pudding, asking if I would like some cream on top. I enthusiastically answered, "I will eat as you eat!" She pulled down a long-ago-opened carton of high-temperature cured cream from the shelf and poured the now lumpy white substance over my pudding. Upon closer inspection, I discovered the cream had become the sticky grave of hundreds of little winged creatures, all too small for my hostess's aging eyes to see. Thinking of Hudson Taylor, the Great Commission and the protein content of insects, I finished the bowl with enthusiasm. When she offered me another bowl, I politely declined and invited her to our eye clinic, hoping she would go before our next meal!

The following day, she did indeed attend our clinic and was thrilled to receive a pair of donated spectacles, restoring her clear vision. I was thrilled that I never saw that box of cream again. Her husband, like most Pitcairners, spends many hours a day making fine handicrafts to sell to visitors and passing ships as well as for mail order. Model replicas of the *Bounty* are a popular item all over the world. I purchased a unique cane with a bird carved on top to take home to my father.

Our projects and fellowship with the islanders continued. We set about to paint the island's only church, built some forty years ago. With brush in hand, Loren kept the team entertained with his anecdotes and jokes accumulated from over two hundred nations that he had visited in his years of missions work.

On Friday morning, I awoke at 4 A.M., my normal time to go on bridge watch. Unable to fall back asleep, I grabbed a flashlight and made my way to the little Seventh-Day Adventist church. Sitting among the drop cloths and painting gear, with the moonlight gently illuminating the sanctuary, I began to speak to the Lord. The feeling of being in this place as part of this historic team was truly overwhelming. This was a phenomenal fulfillment of my vision of a ship in the South Pacific. "Why me?" I once again inquired, full of wonder and gratitude. "Why bring a pastor from the side of a mountain in California, go through all of the hassles of rearranging his life, family and career, to bring him here to this little island? Why bring someone from so far away? Why not someone from Tahiti, or some place closer?"

No sooner had I thought these things than I felt God answering me. "Because I'm extravagant, John. I am willing to make a show of it, a display of My love. It's because I love these people so much that I am willing to rearrange your life and have you bend over backwards to come here. I am bending over backwards to reach out to people and communicate My love. That's why I have brought you here."

In that moment of revelation, I felt an incredible joy and honor that God had chosen me to help bring His love to these people. I didn't mind at all that He had "disrupted" my life and changed my plans so many times. Most of all, I was thankful that I had said yes to Him so many years before and every time since.

That evening, a special service was held for us in the freshly painted church. I was overjoyed to lead the group in singing the praise song based on Isaiah 42:10, which had defined my vision now for seven years. Loren gave a moving message and afterward was presented with a full-size Pitcairn flag. It was one of the most memorable services I have ever attended. I recall missing my family so much and wishing they could be with me to share in the moment. At the feast following the service, I was chatting with a woman whose little baby, Ariel, was about the same age as my daughter Lauren. My heart was touched as the woman allowed me to hold her precious baby.

The next morning, we attended church with the rest of the islanders. The pastor was an Australian man, serving a two-year term with the Seventh-Day Adventist church. To serve on Pitcairn, either he or his wife had to be a registered nurse. In this case, the pastor's wife was a nurse and therefore the island's official medical officer. The pastor and his wife had come to Pitcairn two years ago and had recently volunteered to stay for another term because of their deep love for the people of Pitcairn. I pondered this extraordinary commitment to a place with so little contact with the outside world. Later I was told of an amazing miracle they had experienced on this island only months before our arrival. Many of Pitcairn's treacherous cliffs are named for people who have fallen to their death from their rocky heights. The pastor's little girl had been playing outside but had wandered away from the yard and fallen from a one-hundred-foot cliff, breaking her skull open on the rocks below. Being the island's only trained medical person and desperate to reach her daughter, the child's mother had tried to scale the cliff but had also fallen and broken her own leg. Island residents came to their rescue and placed them side-by-side in the infirmary. Unable to offer medical care, the islanders rang the town bell and called all of the residents to prayer. As they prayed, the little girl's skull literally closed up before their eyes. Tom Christian, sending out urgent radio requests for help to any passing vessel, was answered by the Russian passenger ship *Maxim Gorky,* which altered its course to Pitcairn and took both mother and child off the island to Tahiti for further medical attention. This recent powerful demonstration had served to assure island inhabitants of God's care and presence on this remote yet unforgotten island.

My heart was heavy as the time for our departure drew near. I wished we could stay longer on this charming island. We said our farewells, hugged and shook hands as the islanders ferried us back to the *Ruby* aboard their longboats. The generous Pitcairners produced, as a parting gift, countless baskets full of freshly baked goods, fruits and vegetables for our sail home. After many trips, the last of our gear and personnel had been loaded back onto the *Ruby.* As Captain Tony weighed anchor and turned the ship back toward Tahiti, the islanders' voices once again rose in powerful Pacific harmony singing, "In the sweet by and by, we shall meet on that beautiful shore..." I was helpless to restrain my tears.

Before long, the motion of the ship sent us scurrying to find our bunks and settle in for another long sail. I resumed my schedule of four-hour bridge watches, twice a day, punctuated by the occasional meal and lots of sleep. The seas leveled out long enough for me to seek Loren's advice about my growing desire to work full-time with Mercy Ships in New Zealand. Loren encouraged me in the idea, and I congratulated him on finally reaching Pitcairn. Ever the visionary, he exhorted me, "Now, we have to narrow the focus and go into every county, every province, every city..." Somehow I was not surprised that God had been able to use this man to accomplish such tremendous things.

We sailed back to Papeete, where many members of the team disembarked and flew back to their homes. We stayed for three enjoyable nights before sailing back to Rarotonga, where I caught my flight back to the United States. I had never been so happy to see my wife and children and to be home. But as Shari and I discussed our future plans, we knew that California would not be our home for much longer.

FIFTEEN

The Land of the Long White Cloud

THE final months of 1991 found Shari and me visiting churches and friends and telling the Pitcairn outreach story. We had been accepted to join the Mercy Ships ministry in the South Pacific as the *Ruby*'s project coordinator. Our plans took shape as numerous individuals committed to supporting us through finances and prayer. All members of Youth With A Mission work as volunteers, raising their own financial support. It was remarkable and humbling to watch as God accomplished the seemingly impossible task of providing for our family of five. In February 1992, after saying tearful good-byes once again to our home, church and relatives in Arnold, our family embarked on a grand adventure. The twelve-hour plane ride was adventure enough for Shari and me, trying to keep the kids occupied and happy. I consoled myself by comparing the relative speed in which we were covering such a vast distance by plane to what it would be like making this same trip on the *Ruby*!

My family was delighted when Aotearoa, "the land of the long white cloud," as New Zealand was named by the indigenous Maori population, came into view. We arrived in the middle of the southern hemisphere's summer months. Although it was the dry season, the rolling countryside of New Zealand was green as far as the eye could see. Sheep did indeed dot every hillside, just as the travel books advertised. We were immediately taken with the beauty and charm of this nation. From the surrounding white-sand beaches to the grassy expanses and the interior snowcapped volcanic peaks, New Zealand seemed to have everything, packed into two islands covering a total of 103,737 square miles. We were even more taken with the friendly, hardy people, whose practical, common sense was in sharp contrast to my eccentric, whimsical California style. New Zealand's total population is 3.3 million, with nearly a quarter of those living in the largest city, Auckland, where our plane finally descended.

From Auckland, we traversed the North Island, arriving in Tauranga on the country's east coast. Situated on the gigantic Bay of Plenty, Tauranga served as the home port for the *Pacific Ruby* and the location of the ship's land-based office. We arrived in the midst of hectic preparations for the upcoming medical and evangelistic outreach to the Tongan islands. I soon found myself in the thick of helping organize the April outreach, along with moving my family into our rental home. We had found a nice house near the beach in the community of Mount Maunganui, just across the harbor from Tauranga. After only a week in New Zealand, Shari noticed an advertisement in the paper for a nearby church, which she suggested we try out the following Sunday. We found the recently established fellowship meeting in a high school auditorium. We took our seats, and the service began with singing. In the middle of the worship, the pastor stopped and pointed to my family. He announced, "You are not going to believe this, but last night God showed me that there would be a tall American guy here with his family sitting right where you are! Are you with YWAM?"

In utter shock, I said, "Yes," and glanced around for the nearest exit.

"Sharon can vouch for me," he continued, motioning toward his wife. "God told me you would be missionaries with YWAM and that you would help us with the church here."

With that phenomenal introduction, Shari and I soon became close friends with Pastor Graeme and Sharon Lauridsen. A sincere and enjoyable couple, the Lauridsens had recently started the church and were pleased to have our assistance in developing a leadership team. I was named a pastor in residence and preached as often as I had enough free time from Mercy Ships.

As we adapted to life in a new country, we quickly came to love the Mercy Ships family. Among the workers from many diverse nations were my "old" friends from the Pitcairn outreach along with quite a few new faces. Shari stayed busy adjusting to life in New Zealand. She began home schooling for the first time with Johnny, who was now six years old. With Angie almost three and Lauren just eight months, there was always plenty going on at our house. Along with performing my other tasks, I was able to spend a week teaching in the onboard Discipleship Training School. This group of students would be sailing with us to spend two months in outreach in Tonga and Western Samoa.

I was excited as the day for departure drew near. I spent as much time as possible with Shari and the kids before going away for another five weeks. I would be going only on the Tonga portion of the outreach, and then I would fly home to Tauranga, and David Cowie, the ministry's director, would trade places with me and be on board for the final month in Samoa. We hoped this plan would prevent our families from being separated any longer than absolutely necessary.

After our six-day sail, the crew came back to life as the ship entered the protected waters of Tonga's largest island, Tongatapu. It was essential to stop first at the country's main island to clear customs and immigration and gain necessary clearances for off-loading our cargo and sending our teams ashore on the smaller, outlying islands. While in the capital city, Nuku'alofa, we hosted a reception on board for local church, civic and government leaders. Unable to accommodate everyone in the ship's main lounge, we arranged tables on the *Ruby*'s upper deck and dined with a magnificent view down on Nuku'alofa and its picturesque harbor. Halfway through the evening, the minister of evangelism from the Methodist church stood up and, with emotion in his voice, said, "Being here tonight, with all of the different denominations represented and yet with all of us eating, working and fellowshiping together, has been like sitting in heaven and looking down on earth."

After two weeks in Nuku'alofa, our DTS students moved off board into the local YWAM base to continue with evangelism and assist in the construction of the fledgling University of the Nations branch campus in Tonga. As the students were departing their cabins, our medical team members were arriving to accompany the ship to the Ha'apai group of Tonga. Sailing nineteen hours north, we came to the first of three tiny, remote islands that we would be visiting. With her mere thirteen-foot draft, the *Ruby* proved her value for work in these often inaccessible islands, gliding through shallow waters abounding with treacherous coral reefs. Anchoring as near to shore as possible, the inflatable landing craft would be our shuttle to and from the island. Although the weather proved uncooperative at this island, Ha'ano, members of our medical team who braved the stormy seas and lashing rain found a woman in her seventies who had been injured in the 1984 cyclone. The woman suffered from severe arthritis and a fractured vertebra and used two old sticks to help her walk. The woman was grateful to be given a walker to improve her mobility. Although many of the islanders suffered with untreatable conditions, Dr. Andrew Clark, the ship's chief medical officer, faithfully prayed for every patient. The power of such prayer would be dramatically proven on the next island we visited.

After several rainy days, we proceeded to our second destination, Ha'afeva island. While making house calls, Dr. Andrew discovered a woman suffering from septicemia, a serious blood infection. Like many islanders in poor health, this woman had resigned herself to a slow death in her small home. After prayer and administering antibiotics, our doctor recommended that she be transported on the next passing boat to the nearest island with a hospital where she could receive proper treatment. Before that boat came, however, the woman began to make a dramatic improvement, which our medical team could attribute only to God's healing power.

Later, a small baby was brought to the island's health clinic. The mother had heard of our medical team's presence and had traveled from a nearby island bringing her very ill child. The lethargic five-month-old had suffered convulsions from an extremely high fever. Dr.

Andrew administered antibiotics to combat the underlying infection but knew the infant's prognosis was poor. The child would not even cry or respond to stimuli. Dr. Andrew prayed for the baby and tried to explain the child's condition to the mother. The next day, the medical team members were met as they waded ashore from the landing craft. The excited mother had returned with her baby, who now showed no signs of illness whatsoever. Our hearts were elated as the mother, holding her now smiling and responsive child, proclaimed, "God has healed my baby!"

Two wheelchairs also found grateful recipients on Ha'afeva. One young man, paralyzed from the waist down, had to be pushed around the island in a wheelbarrow. His new wheelchair allowed him greater freedom and independence. The second wheelchair was given to an elderly stroke victim whose tears of appreciation needed no interpretation.

Our final stop was the island of Nomuka. The reception we received at this island was decidedly different from what we had experienced on the rest of the "Friendly Isles," as Tonga was named by mariners long ago. The health official was reluctant to allow us to perform medical work and refused to accept the supplies we offered even though his dispensary shelves were bare. That night on board the ship, the crew decided to devote the next day, a Saturday, to praying on and for the island. With water bottles and sunscreen in hand, we set out in groups the next morning to prayerfully traverse the island.

The following day, as we went ashore to attend church, we found ourselves the unexpected honored guests at a huge feast after the service. Many speeches, watermelons and lobsters later, the pastor asked us to present the evening service in his church. That night, nearly half of the island's one thousand residents packed the church, the largest attendance in history, according to the Methodist pastor. In addition, our medical personnel were asked to off-load their supplies and even treat a few patients before our departure.

Having completed my month on board the ship, I flew home with a few other crew members as David Cowie arrived to take charge for the remainder of the outreach. The *Ruby* sailed on to the recently cyclone-ravaged Samoan islands to offer medical aid and relief. Cyclone Val had hit Samoa in December 1991, sitting for four days over the island of Savai'i. Reports filtering back to the office described the normally lush, verdant island of Savai'i, now stripped bare of all but the trunks of palm trees, looking like toothpicks bristling up all over the island. Most buildings, including the hospital, lacked roofs. Fresh water was in short supply because of damaged water tanks. To survive the storm, island residents had smashed holes in their concrete water tanks, allowed the water to drain out and sought refuge inside. Some families lived in the confines of their water tanks for days.

In comparison to the excitement of being with the ship on outreach, coming back to the office was similar to being the activities director for a cemetery. Abbe Anderson, the ship's public relations officer who had also flown back from Tonga, and I passed the days by writing reports from the outreach to be published in the various Mercy Ships newsletters and traveling to churches around New Zealand's North Island to raise awareness about the ministry and needs of the Pacific islands.

With joy we welcomed the *Ruby* and her crew back to Tauranga a month later and soon began preparations for the next Discipleship Training School and island medical outreach. I was left to organize the outreach as David and Linda Cowie flew to the States to appear on the Christian TV show *The 700 Club*.

In October, we were bid bon voyage as we set sail for a return visit to the Ha'apai group of Tonga. This time, we visited the hospital on Lifuka, the largest of the Ha'apai islands, and made follow-up trips to Ha'afeva and Nomuka. We concentrated on evangelism and eye work, distributing 420 pairs of reading glasses. Tonga's only ophthalmologist, Dr. Afu Taumoepeau, accompanied the ship to the outer Ha'apai group and reported, "We've done a lot toward the prevention of blindness, thanks to people like you who have come to help us."

Being back in the islands of Tonga was a fulfilling time for me. I found that God had made a special place in my heart for these people. Once again, I found their generous, friendly culture to be enjoyable and refreshing and as beautiful as the magnificent islands they call home. I gazed with appreciation at the islands God had surrounded with sparkling waters and turquoise reefs. With every bountiful feast, served to us with extravagant hospitality, I gave thanks to God for teaching me more about Himself and His abundant provision.

I was extremely pleased as we sailed into Nomuka's pristine waters and received a much warmer reception than we had on our previous visit. This time our work and presence were welcomed. Children crowded around us with delight as we took time to play games with them. They were fascinated by our puppets and balloons, which many of them had never seen before, and giggled as we tried to play ball and jump rope with them. One little boy literally fell to the ground laughing as we painstakingly tried to learn to sing "Jesus Loves Me" in Tongan.

Our engineers also came ashore to repair countless generators and outboard motors. On islands where fish is a staple of the diet and interisland transport depends on boats, repairing outboards is a vital service.

Members of our evangelism team accompanied an island pastor on home visits. The pastor took our team to the house of one man who had been traumatized a decade earlier by a surgery without anesthetic. Since the surgery, the man had spent his days sitting speechless on the floor in the corner of his family's home. Our team devoted the entire day to him, praying and reading scriptures. They returned to his house on the second day and again spent the day encouraging him and telling him the gospel story. By the end of the second day, the man had begun to talk and had prayed to receive Jesus as his Savior. He was overwhelmed that the team had spent so much time with him expressing God's love and devotion. As the ship was preparing to depart the island, our team had to leave the man's home and bid him farewell. The man asked them to wait as he was slowly helped to his feet and made his way outside into the sunshine to have his picture taken with the team. He and his family were grateful, and the whole community was amazed.

The month in Tonga went quickly, and we soon found ourselves braving the six-day sail back to New Zealand. Our stay in Tauranga was brief, as we began a public relations tour of South Island in December, sailing to the ports of Nelson, Dunedin and Invercargill.

Shari and I found it hard to believe we had completed nearly a full year with Mercy Ships. With the preparation from one outreach flowing into the next, it seemed like there was never a dull moment.

Our second year in New Zealand proved to be equally busy and interesting. We began planning for our next scheduled outreaches to

Tonga, Fiji, Papua New Guinea and the Solomon Islands. The stress on personnel and resources that would come from such a demanding schedule led to the decision to change our original plans and shorten our outreach circuit to include Tonga, Fiji and perhaps one of the nearer islands of the Vanuatu chain. None of us knew the real significance of this vital change in our destination. As we proceeded with our preparations, we were unaware that God had long ago arranged an appointment at which our attendance was decidedly required.

SIXTEEN

Gold on the Water

I HAD never experienced such difficulties in organizing an outreach. The ship was scheduled to depart for Tonga in April, and I was getting nowhere with the preparations. My main problem was Fijian bureaucracy. It seemed there were miles upon miles of government red tape to be waded through to visit any outlying Fijian islands. Finally, Shari and I flew to Nadi to work things out in person. We drove from Nadi along the southern coastal route to Suva and connected with the local YWAM base. We met Kasa, a bright young Fijian woman who was home on furlough from the *Anastasis*, the largest vessel of the Mercy Ships fleet. Kasa graciously offered her expert assistance in making the necessary arrangements for the *Ruby*'s visit, and by the time we left Fiji a week later, we felt we had made good progress. There were still a few loose ends that Kasa would attend to, and I would keep in touch with her on how things were progressing.

Being distracted with the Fijian matters, I neglected to pay much attention to the preparations that seemed to be falling right into place for our time in Vanuatu or to the reports from Dr. Andrew and Graeme, who had flown to Tanna to do some advance work. The two men had received assurance of necessary government clearance and reported a suitable wharf at Lenakel on Tanna. They had visited "custom villages" and heard about a cargo cult, but any significance to their stories was lost in my preoccupied brain. I was just happy to set sail from Tauranga in April and trust that all was in order.

As the ship tossed and rolled her way to Tonga, I reflected over the past twenty years of my life. In a few days it would be Easter Sunday. This year was special to me, as it marked the twenty-year anniversary from that Easter in San Andreas when I gave up my plans and said yes to God's calling into ministry. I was disappointed that we would be back at sea on Easter Sunday, sailing from Tonga to Fiji. I had hoped I would have the chance to preach on this personally significant day. I remember talking it over with God and deciding it wasn't worth fretting over. Finally I prayed, "Lord, let us have something exciting happen on this outreach. Let's have an adventure!"

Normally I know better than to make such requests. No sooner had I prayed than the ship's engine died. We were three days out of Tauranga, three days from Tonga, right in the middle of nowhere! Furthermore, Captain Jesse was keeping a close eye on regular weather faxes we were receiving that showed a threatening weather system curving our way. We had been hoping to make good time and get north of the path of this potential cyclone, but now it looked like we could be in trouble. Our engineers worked tirelessly for nearly twelve hours to execute midocean repairs. We were all amazed and thankful that the seas remained remarkably calm during those hours, as our helpless little vessel was literally at the mercy of the waves.

We sent word back to Tauranga by radio, requesting prayer support. Our combined prayer efforts were miraculously answered as the weather faxes showed the cyclonic system making an uncharacteristic turn. In fact, had we made good time and not had to stop for engine repairs, we would have ended up right in its path. Once again under way, we limped into Tonga's harbor and docked at Queen Salote wharf. David Cowie and John Brignall, our marine superintendent, made an emergency flight into Tonga, bringing their expertise and replacement parts. Our scheduled overnight stay in Nuku'alofa turned into a longer visit as repairs were made on the engine, ensuring the safety and success of the rest of the voyage.

I was delighted to see Pastor Tony Fuamoano, who came down to the dock as soon as he heard we had arrived. Pastor Tony had been instrumental in organizing our first and second outreaches to Tonga and had allowed our teams to minister in his church, Victory Assembly of God. Upon learning that we would be in town for a few days, Pastor Tony graciously invited me to preach at all three of the Easter services at his church.

I rarely understand the mysterious ways in which God works, but I knew that God had seen the desire of my heart and heard my reckless prayer. What I didn't know was that this was only the beginning of an incredible adventure.

After completing engine repairs and ministry in Tonga, we sailed on to Fiji. As usual, our first port of call would be the capital, Suva, where we would clear customs and immigration and receive clearance to visit the outer island of Vanua Levu, where our medical help and relief supplies were most needed. My hopes that the bureaucratic red tape had all been taken care of by my earlier visit here were soon shattered. The ship's purser Jenni and I spent hours traveling across town from one government office to the next, only to be sent back to the first office again. The official assurance we had been given before our arrival that the normal fees for customs and immigration would be waived in light of our charitable status seemed to evaporate into thin air. Finally we were informed that we would be allowed to donate our cargo to their outlying islands only under supervision. They would send two customs officials with us to oversee the delivery, but we would be required to pay a large fee, along with other levies, to cover the two men's salaries. Disappointed with this development and exhausted from the heat and rigmarole, Jenni and I returned to the ship. I was not pleased with this condition, nor did I have a large budget to cover this unforeseen expense. The cash we had on board was for the crew's food and the purchase of fresh water and other necessities.

That evening I stood on the bow of the ship, gazing across the harbor toward the bright yellow lights on the wharf. I was feeling inclined to forget sailing on to the outer island and just take our help else-where, maybe sail to Vanuatu ahead of schedule. But that wouldn't work, because several of our team members were scheduled to fly into Fiji to join the ship. Besides, there was much to be done in Vanua Levu. Earnestly I asked God for help in making this decision. I did not want to deplete the ship's cash supply and run us into bigger trouble later on. As I pondered the dilemma, I noticed the reflection of the shore lights sparkling on the water. It looked like millions of gold coins being flung out over the peaceful harbor, scattering their way to the very edge of the ship. I was suddenly ashamed of my irritation and apprehension about the situation. I knew God was saying to me, "John, do I not have all the resources in this universe at my disposal? Can I not provide for you? Do what I sent you here to do." Feeling gently reprimanded, I said a prayer of repentance and retired for the night. I knew now what to do.

The next morning, Jenni and I accepted the government conditions and prepared to receive the two customs agents on board for the sail to Vanua Levu. The two men were obviously curious about the nature of our work, and we were happy to answer all their questions. Of the two, one was a Christian who seemed supportive of our efforts, and the other man, Viliame, although not a believer, was very interested and expressed his enjoyment of the family atmosphere on board the *Ruby*.

Upon arrival in Vanua Levu, we were excited to find that the local church had been busily and expectantly preparing for our teams. The people had a huge tent erected near the dock and a long series of meetings scheduled every night for over a week. I breathed a sigh of relief as I thought of the disappointment we would have caused had I canceled our plans to come here at the last minute.

The agents observed as we off-loaded donated clothing, soup mix and the other supplies we had brought. A portion of our team moved ashore. They would be staying here for three weeks while the ship sailed to other ports. At the final evangelistic meeting before the ship was to return to Suva, every crew member was elated as Viliame came forward at the invitation to receive Christ as his Savior! As I thought of the gold on the water, I realized that a few days' wages were in fact a small price to pay for this man's eternal salvation. To God, the man was priceless.

Sailing back to Suva, we bid fond farewells to our new customs friends and at the same time received the additional members of our crew who had flown into Fiji. Graeme Butler, an Australian optometrist, joined us, as did Abbe, our writer and photographer, and a new recruit, Diane Hetfield, who would be helping with the photography and gaining her first experience with Youth With A Mission. Graeme Butler brought 333 pounds of excess baggage from Tasmania, including over one thousand pairs of reading glasses and a sophisticated, computerized refractometer capable of evaluating a person's visual acuity in just fifteen seconds. The use of this machine brought the most up-to-date eye care available in the world to the people of Tanna. As the final members arrived and the ship's complement was complete, we departed Fijian waters bound for Vanuatu. The rest of our medical team, including Dr. Andrew, dentist Charlie Roberts and his team and Dr. Steve Morris, an infectious disease specialist from New Zealand, would be meeting us in Vanuatu.

By this time, I was longing for home. I was counting the days until I would be relieved by David and I could fly back to New Zealand and to my family. I had only a few more days at sea, a short stop in Port Vila for government clearance, then a one-week, hopefully uneventful outreach in which I would be conducting a pastors conference—something familiar that I could do well. I settled into my bunk, comforting myself with the knowledge that nothing extraordinary could possibly happen in one short week on the tiny island of Tanna. I was neglecting to take into account that for God, one week is enough time to make a world of difference.

As we neared our destination and our prayer teams began to report repeated guidance to scriptures referring to John the Baptist's ministry, I began to anticipate a fruitful time of evangelism. My expectations, however, certainly did not reach the level of what God was about to unfold. I never imagined that the coming week was destined to be of such significance. But before the week had passed, armed with only my little Bible and a bird perched curiously upon my head, I had been catapulted into the strangest events of my life, befriending a formidable island chief, being mistaken for some sort of island legend and coming face-to-face with a forbidding volcano and island culture.

As if all this were not enough, by the end of the week when I thought my peculiar association with these people and their island was almost completed, God was planning otherwise. As I was flying home, God was preparing to reveal even more of His remarkable love and design for these people. My work here was only just beginning.

PART THREE

"We Will Live Forever
When John Frum Comes"

SEVENTEEN

Struggling to Return

SINCE my return to New Zealand following my first visit to Tanna, the John Frum people were never far from my thoughts. My desire to help Chief Isaak and his people simmered in my mind. I longed to return. I wanted to see my friends there again. I wanted to encourage Isaak and see what our first visit had really meant, if anything.

I wrote to Loren Cunningham to describe the John Frum contact and ask for his advice. I requested that he assign more capable help. He promptly replied, saying Dr. Charlie Roberts had already informed him of the contact and that he felt I had handled it with wisdom. He further encouraged me, saying he felt my work on the *Ruby* was only a "stepping stone to greater ministry in the Pacific."

In October, I had the opportunity to meet with Tom Hallas, YWAM's director for Asia and the Pacific, at John and Stephanie Lindeman's beautiful harborside home in Auckland. Since our CDTS, John and I had kept in close touch. John and Stephanie had even come with the *Ruby* on our first outreach to Tonga. Over dinner, John and Steph encouraged me to tell the Tanna story. Tom, a veteran missionary with years of experience in Melanesia and a broad knowledge of cargo cults, listened with interest. The next morning, Tom hurried down to the kitchen and excitedly shared how he had been stirred by the Lord during the night that the John Frum contact was a vital work of God among these people.

The encouragement and enthusiasm from others spurred my own desire to make a return visit to Tanna. I was torn, though, between the idea of a "greater ministry in the Pacific" and my fear of being in over my head. In addition, it was not looking likely that the New Zealand government would enable us to remain in the country. Our application for residency had not yet been granted, and our work visas were soon to expire. We found ourselves in a predicament many overseas missionaries face. Our future ministry in the Pacific was uncertain as a result of political and economic issues over which we had no control. We were keenly aware of and thankful for the prayers of our friends, family and church who supported us as we sought the Lord's will for our family's future. We knew that God was in control, but for whatever reason, He had not yet shared with us the final outcome.

We pondered whether God was perhaps leading us in a new direction, away from New Zealand. Shari and I decided to look into other avenues of ministry in case our application for residency was denied. We had contacted Christian Associates International (CAI) and were interested in its church-planting efforts in Europe. Living in New Zealand had given us an introduction to European culture, and we felt drawn to learn more. We scheduled our family's return to the USA in April 1994 to include visits to several states, speaking and catching up with friends, family and supporters before making our way to Europe. We would also meet and interview with the leadership of CAI in California. And so, as we waited, we lived in a tension between the possibility of being able to continue our work in the Pacific and our excitement about the emerging opportunities to be of service in Europe.

In the meantime, we were busy with our own church-planting efforts. I concluded my work with Mercy Ships, recording a number of radio spots to be aired on a Christian station long after we would leave the country. Our church, Bay Christian Life Centre, had just started a new church in Papamoa, a nearby, rapidly growing family community. Pastor Graeme Lauridsen and I shared the preaching and pastoral load of the two churches until a full-time pastor could be found for the Papamoa church.

As I described the events in Tanna, these two congregations began to rally around the John Frum people and their needs. They adopted the John Frum people as a prayer and ministry focus and began to raise funds for my return visit. It was quite a blessing as these congregations recognized the vital part that they could play in reaching and discipling thousands of people living so differently and distantly from themselves.

As we struggled to work out the timing for my follow-up visit, we prayed for the Lord to work sovereignly among these special people. Our primary prayer was that the wall of prejudice between the John Frum followers and the church in Tanna would be brought down and that the chief and local pastors would become strong allies in the work of reaching Frum villages. If this openness and cooperation developed, it might not be necessary to send in an American outsider. We really felt that the best thing would be for the Tannese to reach out to one another.

But I knew of the years of animosity that existed between the Frum people and their own Vanuatu countrymen, including their Christian neighbors. Just over a decade ago, when the newly independent country was rallying around its newfound national identity, the John Frum people, out of allegiance to America, refused to fly the Vanuatu flag. Having lived through the Vietnam era, when the Stars and Stripes was being burned and denounced, I knew the anger and resentment that that kind of protest produces. If the Tannese factions could be brought together by Jesus Christ, it would be a powerful testimony of reconciliation.

Our other major request was that the Lord would open up a non-Presbyterian connection to Chief Isaak One and his people. The Presbyterian leaders who were so instrumental in our initial contact were regarded with suspicion by many of the Frum people. It was the Presbyterian church that had initially controlled the island and had aggressively oppressed early John Frum efforts. In my first visit, the Presbyterian leaders themselves, out of concern for John Frum evangelism, encouraged me to find some other channels to work through. They explained that if the Frum people saw me as a Presbyterian representative, it could harm my effectiveness. When my good friend architect Greg Dryden accepted an invitation to dinner at our home, he unknowingly brought the answer to these prayers with him.

Greg had been a student on board the *Ruby* during the outreach to Tanna and had played a vital role in the initial John Frum contact, delivering the evangelism message at Sulphur Bay. As we took time over dinner to catch up on each other's lives, the conversation turned to Tanna. Greg spoke of his frustration at not being able to complete a project he had begun while in Tanna. He had lent his expertise as an architect to the Assembly of God church in Lenakel. The people there were working hard to finish and roof their large new church building. Greg had worked out many of the design details but was in need of some further onsite information and help with funding the purchase of building supplies. I later learned that Pastor Nathan had been very active in reaching out to the John Frum people, especially since the openness that our visit had created.

As a result of Greg's and my conversation and subsequent contacts with Pastor Nathan in Lenakel, the Bay Christian Life Centres began to raise funds for this church roofing project. Through our personal newsletter "New Song," Shari and I presented the project to our supporters and asked for their help. I was intrigued to learn that Pastor Nathan was related by marriage to Chief Isaak and that the two men had a trust in each other. With this contact through the Assembly of God in Tanna, God had given us the new and more appropriate channel that we had requested. At the same time, He had answered Greg's prayer for help in fulfilling his promise to his island friends.

My own commitment to return was being sorely tested. When it seemed that everything was coming together for me to leave for Tanna in December 1993, I became ill with a series of respiratory infections, culminating in pneumonia. It was the longest bout with illness that I have ever had. For nearly two months, in the middle of the New Zealand summer, I was struggling with my unseasonable ailment, changing antibiotics and coughing through the night. Not knowing the status of our visa application, I found my weary thoughts further consumed with all of the arrangements that would have to be made before our departure. In a very short time, if the visas did not come through, we would need to sell our home and car and pack up all of our belongings.

It was a time of spiritual battles and intercessions as we wrestled against a few dark opponents. It was hard to avoid the conclusion that there were forces at work that did not want our contact with Tanna to continue. As our April departure for the USA approached, my hope of revisiting Tanna began to fade. At last, as my health slowly improved, I made a final attempt to arrange my second visit to Tanna in March.

Shortly before I was scheduled to fly to Vanuatu, I received a very special package from my Mercy Ships friend Abbe Anderson. Abbe had gone home to Colorado to spend the Christmas holidays with her family and had reported the John Frum contact story to her supporting churches and friends.

After hearing Abbe tell the story, Larry Leek, a friend with an exceptional memory, recalled reading about the John Frum people in a *National Geographic*. The next day, after locating a copy in his basement, Larry brought the May 1974 edition of *National Geographic* to Abbe. In it was a remarkable, twenty-year-old account entitled, "A Pacific Island Awaits Its Messiah: Tanna Awaits the Coming of John Frum." The pictures, now two decades old, of islanders with USA painted in red across their chests, marching with bamboo rifles, sitting on the volcano's rim and bowing before a giant red cross had been taken about the time I became a Christian and said yes to God's call to be a pastor.

For me, the article, along with the providential way in which it had come to light, was a much-needed encouragement and confirmation. I could hardly wait to show the pictures to Isaak and ask what he recalled about the photojournalist's visit so long ago.

In addition to the magazine, I had another special gift for Isaak— a battery-operated cassette player with a blank tape. While on Tanna, I would arrange to have a portion of Scripture interpreted into the chief's language and recorded onto the tape. I felt it would be good to start with the opening chapters of John, in that they clearly describe the relationship and roles of Jesus Christ and John the Baptist. I knew that Isaak and others would listen to this over and over and that it would help to lay a foundation for the proper reinterpretation of the John Frum figure. I was excited, as their own prophetess had clearly associated John Frum with John the Baptist. I prayed that these scriptures would reveal that like John the Baptist, John Frum's purpose was to introduce the true Savior, Jesus Christ.

As I began my interisland flight from Port Vila to Tanna, I noticed the tall, fit Tannese man sitting opposite me on the small plane. We were both struggling to find room for our long legs in the hopelessly hot and cramped cabin. I struck up a conversation and learned that he was Mr. Song, the member of parliament chosen by Isaak One to represent the John Frum people. I was excited to learn that he too was related to Pastor Nathan and had recently begun to attend a nearby Assembly of God church. He seemed equally excited to meet me and obviously remembered my previous visit. I realized that God was again providing wonderful bridges into the Frum leadership.

As we landed on the rolling grass strip on Tanna, we were greeted by Pastor Nathan and Chief Isaak. The two men drove us down the hill into Lenakel, where we continued our visit outside the unfinished Assembly of God church. After making our arrangements for the week's activities, I walked the short path through the bush to the co-op store and on down to the wharf, where we had brought the *Ruby* alongside just ten months earlier. To my astonishment, the not-long-ago constructed concrete wharf had been totally destroyed by a recent hurricane. The seas had been so violent that the large concrete retainers, eight feet across and resembling large jacks, had been blown out of place and were strewn like a child's toys along the shoreline. A beautiful old home that had overlooked the cove for years was now completely gone. I wondered whether God had placed that wharf there for one appointment—the visit of our white ship less than a year earlier and the opportunity to fulfill a people's expectations.

EIGHTEEN

"John Frum Gave
Us This Cross"

O N my first night in Tanna, Pastor Nathan's church presented a wonderful feast. Life on Tanna goes on much as it has for generations. Small villages of related families are hidden throughout the
island bush. The families live a cooperative lifestyle in their small and
artfully constructed thatched huts. The women and small children
spend most of their days around the cooking huts, which are about
eight to ten feet on a side with a stone-rimmed fire on the dirt floor.
The women sit on woven mats around the fire as they roll out and prepare their taro root and sweet potato delicacies on wide green leaves.
There may be a small shelf on the wall for washing and storing pots
and dishes. The hard-working women of Tanna can be seen with large
bundles of firewood hung from their forehead and down their back or
with heavy jugs of water in hand. The older children amuse themselves
by playing in the nearby bush or along the seashore.

It is customary for the women to bring the prepared meals to
another hut where the men will gather and eat. There is little talk

between men and women except for the private discussions of husbands and wives. The diet on Tanna is simple—often a bowl of rice with a vegetable soup poured over and bits of chicken, beef or fish on top. This is usually accompanied by a generous supply of taro, sweet potato and fried breads. When the men have finished, the food is returned to the cooking hut, where the women and children eat what is left and prepare for the next meal or feast. In the middle of the village is a clearing, where the chief meets regularly with the men to exchange stories and make community decisions.

On Tanna, the chief's word is law, and the chief is involved in all manner of public and private affairs. A wife who leaves her husband because of drunkenness or abuse will retreat to her family's village. The chief there will work to resolve the problem through negotiation, the imposition of fines or public humiliation. This kind of community shame is a powerful corrective force, considering just about everyone is related.

As the welcoming feast and evening ended, I retired to my small room and thin foam mattress under the protection of a draped mosquito net. The tropical heat and humidity were intense. Even the islanders were complaining! The night seemed long.

Early the next morning, I dressed in my lava-lava and began my work. I spent the morning measuring the church building so as to have accurate information for Greg to plan the roof design. As the afternoon sun grew hotter, I finished my measurements and made my way down to the beach. As I waded in the cooling ocean waters, suddenly my ankle collapsed when a large stone was rolled up by the surf onto my foot. Over the next couple of days, my swollen ankle grew more painful. My hosts became concerned that I had broken something inside my foot and encouraged me to visit the village "doctor."

Finally, Pastor Nathan said he would take me to get some medicine. As we slowly walked through the bush along the shore to a clearing of huts, Pastor Nathan explained how so many of the plants on Tanna have healing properties. He said that their village doctor had learned from his father how to use them. "He knows exactly how to fix broken bones," I was assured.

We were led into a small hut where the medicine man was preparing some brew on the fire. Pastor Nathan introduced me and described my problem to the doctor, who listened intently and glanced at me. Holding up an open jar containing a yellow liquid, he began, "This is how we can heal your foot.

"We will cut your foot open with a knife," he explained as he held up a sharpened piece of bamboo, "pour in some of this medicine, wrap it up for four weeks, and it will be good again."

He called out the door, and a young girl came in. The man held out the girl's forearm and showed me a six-inch scar where the bone had clearly been broken and had healed with a small but noticeable angle. He said, "This girl had a broken bone, but we cut her open, poured in the medicine and wrapped her up. Now she is good again."

I tried to look impressed but cringed inside as I thought of the pain the girl must have experienced. I shook the doctor's hand and, as graciously and politely as possible, replied, "I thank you very much for wanting to help me, but I will go home very soon, and I will ask my own medicine man to help me." I had never before missed the doctors on board the ship more than I did at that moment! I left the "doctor's" hut with a new appreciation for the lack of proper medical care that these islanders endure.

I hobbled back to my shady afternoon perch and put my swollen ankle up on a pillow. Out of my open-air window I saw an old man arrive. The man was leading a goat and carrying two large baskets, each cleverly woven out of a single whole palm frond and filled with fruits and vegetables. I watched as Pastor Nathan went out to greet him and was stunned as the man took a large machete and quickly cut the goat's throat. The scene was quite new to me. I looked away as the men exchanged farewells and the visitor departed, leaving the lifeless beast bleeding on the ground.

Nathan called a number of the men to the scene, and together they hung the goat from a limb, burned off its hair with torches and set about to butcher the meat. We had another big feast that night as Nathan explained that the old man's wife had recently become ill and died. Nathan had helped the family through their grief, and the man had come with these gifts of gratitude.

The next morning, Pastor Nathan and Manu, a sharp young elder in the church, announced it was time for them to show me their "special treasure." A small truck arrived. Several men piled into the bed of the pickup, and I was placed in the passenger seat as we left for a long, rough ride along the coast to the southern end of the island. As we bounced over the rocky track, I admired the beauty of this coastline with its untouched black-sand beaches and crashing waves. Small seaside villages were the only occasional interruption to the natural scene. After about forty minutes, we left the coast and began a very slow and difficult trip into the bush, climbing into the island's mountainous interior. We had reached the Green Point area, site of some of the oldest John Frum villages. This is where John Frum was said to have made his first appearances.

In the 1930s, when the Presbyterian church was forcefully suppressing the islanders' culture and way of life, the mysterious figure began to meet with villagers here under the cover of night, wearing a large hat to disguise himself. Some of John's earliest statements were that the church was good, the Bible was good but their customs were also good.

This message, which today would be quite acceptable to modern missionary understanding, was the cause of great upheaval for Tanna's society. The villagers, who were virtually all at least nominally Christian at that time, found this concept to be of great encouragement to their growing protests of the church's Tanna laws, which forbade their traditional way of life. As increasing numbers of Tannese began to defy the laws and to practice their customs again, the church reacted with brutal discipline, disrupting villages, incarcerating the leaders and even binding followers on poles and forcibly bringing them to church.

It was at this time that the statements of John supposedly took a more defiant tone. John is said to have declared that the Tannese were to remove their children from the Presbyterian-operated schools, leave the churches and return to their former way of life. John promised that someday a better religion would come to Tanna, but until then, they were to wait.

The Tannese rallied around these words, and in one of the most remarkable episodes in cultural history, practically everyone joined the John Frum movement, nailing the church doors shut and expelling the church leaders. As this movement was at its height, the American forces came with all their machinery, medicine, technology and supplies. The

Americans, both black and white, were generous and kind to the people of Tanna, distributing and caring freely for them and paying them in greenbacks.

This age of generosity and plenty was accompanied by a new "religious" custom. The Tannese observed the marching formations, chain of command, discipline, reveille, taps and especially the ceremony surrounding the flag as it was raised and lowered with such pageantry. Surely this was the new religion that John Frum America had promised.

But when the Pacific war was over, the American era of abundance ended and left only the remnants of a faraway world. The John Frum people, feeling that they had somehow disappointed the American heaven and its gods, endeavored to win back its favor by keeping the new customs alive. If they stayed true to the rituals, to the flag, to whatever America might be, surely John would return with all the previous benefits and more. The people need not work or educate their children. They need only wait and hold faithfully to their beliefs. This had made it difficult for the John Frum people to progress over the past half century.

As we continued through the thick bush, we emerged into a clearing on the top of a hill. There were six large huts set inside a tidy fence and nearly a hundred Frum children playing in the field.

"This is Iakamhau, our 'Star School,' our treasure!" Pastor Nathan announced proudly. "We opened this school just two months ago, and now these children are coming from the oldest John Frum villages to learn English, basic studies and the Bible for the first time. This is the fruit of your last visit. Frum chiefs, their people and their children are coming to school and to the church!"

I was thrilled and humbled to see the eager students and teachers in their thatched classrooms, seated on logs and writing on narrow split timber benches. On the low walls were small bits of blackboard with vocabulary words and math problems. Each student had a basket with his meager supplies and books and a short length of bamboo, like a cup, holding his pencils. The island of Tanna has about seven indigenous languages, many of them unwritten. Since the Frum people are eager to learn the "American" language, this kind of bush school is a vital way to educate, disciple and make the Bible accessible to them.

Chief Isaak's remarkable openness had unlocked a floodgate, allowing what had been banned among the John Frum people for over fifty years.

"We have teachers and students. But because of the rain and cold in the mountains here, we have to redo the thatched roof on these huts every nine months," Pastor Nathan explained. "If you could help us to build permanent buildings and to get more supplies, we could fill many more classrooms and many more schools with John Frum children."

As we toured the school I was struck at how so many people could be reached at so little cost. These children will soon be the best-educated young leaders among the John Frum people. As we loaded back into the truck and returned to Lenakel, I realized how in this way the opportunity existed to disciple the entire people group and bring them a new hope for the future through Jesus Christ.

By now, a local man had recorded the first section of the Gospel of John onto my cassette tape, and I was looking forward to our visit with Isaak One the next day. Pastors Nathan, Willy and James had all given me exciting reports about how John Frum chiefs and people had been coming to Jesus and were being baptized in unprecedented numbers. Their many positive reports were quite encouraging, but as we made our way over the central mountains toward Sulphur Bay, I was filled with anticipation and some anxiety as to what my visit with Isaak One would hold.

My anxieties were quickly relieved as we arrived to another wonderful welcome from the village. Chief Isaak and I were both excited to spend time with each other and exchange stories. I presented Isaak with the cassette player and tape, and then I opened the *National Geographic* to show him the pictures. I asked, "Do you remember when the people were here taking these pictures? Your people are very famous! People all over the world have seen these photos. Do you recognize any of these people?"

Isaak said that he remembered when the camera people had come. He looked intently at the article's leading picture, with Frum men marching in formation. He pointed to various ones and said, "This man is a chief now. This man is dead. This man is me, Chief Isaak One!"

I marveled as he pointed to the stern-faced fifth man in line wearing gray trousers. It was Isaak! So young looking. "My friend in the *National Geographic*," I remarked with pride.

We began to walk together with our interpreter across the parade grounds. I could tell that my friend had changed. He told me that since our first visit, he had invited a group of Vanuatu evangelists to spend a month in his village. The Every Home Vanuatu team of four had spent their time evangelizing and discipling the chief and his people. I was thrilled to hear of this new openness to the church, but I was ready to dance, even with my painful ankle, when he said, "It is time for us to work together with the church so that everyone can know Jesus and everyone can go to heaven."

With excitement, I said, "You are right, Chief. That is a very good decision."

We then walked into the John Frum church. At one end of the small, unadorned and unfurnished thatched hut stood the large red cross of John Frum with flowers scattered around its base. A relic from the medics of World War II, this symbol had for over half a century represented the hope of the John Frum people that one day "America" would come back to save them. I pointed to the large red cross and inquired, "What does this cross mean to you now?"

The chief smiled and responded slowly and sincerely, "John Frum gave us this cross, but it is the cross that Jesus died on for us, and that is what I want my people to know."

I was overjoyed and filled with gratitude to God for answering our prayers and breaking down the barriers on Tanna. I felt confident that the Tannese Christians would be able to reach out to the Frum people and win them to Jesus. The miracle of reconciliation was beginning.

We left Sulphur Bay and returned to Lenakel. My visit to Tanna was nearly finished. Pastor Nathan was delighted by Isaak's words and desire to work with the church. He and the other pastors seemed even more amazed than I was at the chief's continued openness. They talked excitedly about the many opportunities and possibilities and the best way to work together to help the John Frum people. I smiled as I realized that God was working just as dramatic a change in the hearts of these pastors as He had among the John Frum people.

At my farewell service in the makeshift church in front of the unfinished new building, Pastor Nathan presented me with a very special gift. He held out a simple wooden cross and said, "Pastor Rush, this is for you. It is to commemorate the time when the red cross of John Frum became the cross of Jesus Christ."

I have received many more expensive and elaborate gifts, but none has ever been more gratifying.

NINETEEN

"To an Unknown God"

AS soon as my plane landed in New Zealand, my family and I began the chaotic project of packing up our lives and preparing for our extended time away. Our residency visas had at last been granted, but we had already committed to a ministry and speaking schedule in the USA and Europe. For the time being, we decided to rent out our home and car in Mt. Maunganui instead of selling them. We still had to pack up all of our belongings and put the majority into storage.

My visit to Tanna had encouraged me that the growing cooperation between church and John Frum leaders was the key to reaching the Frum people. This would minimize their dependence on outside involvement, especially mine! I had almost convinced myself that my very strange role there, and thus my obligation, was coming to an end.

In addition, we were genuinely looking forward to our upcoming visit with Linus Morris and the Christian Associates team. We had some longtime mutual ties with CAI and were excited about the possibility of pastoring a newly founded church in Hoofdorp, near Amsterdam.

In spite of the encouragement I had received from Loren Cunningham, Tom Hallas and others about further work in Tanna and the Pacific, I was reluctant to pursue it. I had no clue how to handle this kind of thing. It is not routinely taught in the seminaries. I was thrilled at what had occurred, but I was afraid that my continued involvement might inadvertently muddle the whole thing up. In truth, I wanted to flee. I was hoping to play a far more familiar role as church planter in a somewhat more familiar culture about as far away from Tanna as one could get.

We arrived in San Francisco in late April and had a wonderful reunion with friends and family. After a couple of weeks, we made our way south to Thousand Oaks, where we had a marvelous time meeting the CAI team and speaking to some of the leaders we hoped to be working with in Europe. But as we visited and exchanged stories with our friends and fellow ministry workers, it was clear to see that our hearts were still in the Pacific. When the time would come to speak about our opportunities in Europe, we would often end up telling about our Pacific vision instead. The entire CAI staff listened intently as we told the story of the Frum contact. I think they knew that we would not be settling in Europe.

We spent the next couple of weeks in agonizing prayer over which side of the globe God wanted us to be on. Finally, we resolved to return to the Pacific, with all of its uncertainties, so as to see that the John Frum contact was followed up. But we would need help. We prayed that God would give us mature, capable and discerning partners for the challenging work ahead. Content with our decision, we further resolved to complete our already arranged tour of the USA and Europe before returning to New Zealand. It would be our first opportunity in a long time to see many of our old friends and tell the John Frum story.

We visited our close friends Jack and Kay Rudd, who had moved to Utah and held key roles in the Salt Lake Christian Fellowship. The Rudds had been working tirelessly to encourage the congregation and lead the church-operated primary and secondary school through major growth and development. Their experience gained from pioneering our Christian school in Arnold had proved invaluable.

That June's graduation ceremonies were going to be quite special for the Salt Lake Christian Fellowship and for Jack and Kay personally. The Rudds' son Jay would be graduating and receiving his high school diploma. I had known Jay from our first gathering on that rainy and muddy day in 1978 in the Rudds' home in the forests near Arnold, California. Jay had been a small and struggling Down syndrome child surrounded by his loving parents and proud brothers, Aaron and Dion. Jack and Kay, along with the church's senior pastor, Corky Seevinck, asked whether I would be available to speak at the commencement ceremony and at their church services on Sunday. I was honored to accept. It was one of the highlights of my ministry career to speak at Jay Rudd's graduation.

We had an enjoyable time with the Rudds. Jay's special day became a hearth around which we were able to exchange so many stories, old and new, about how our lives and families had grown. The Rudds' church family embraced us warmly and responded generously to our Pacific vision. One morning over coffee, Jack revealed that they had been feeling the Lord directing them to work with us, but he didn't know whether they would be the right people for the task. I was thrilled to hear that God was calling this special couple to be our partners. I excitedly told them how we believed that the fostering of Christian schools and churches in Frum villages was the best way to disciple these special people. The Rudds' considerable background in education was perfect preparation for the task. In addition, Jack's years of experience in trade and business would be vital to expanding the ministry efforts. I couldn't think of anyone I would rather have on the team!

As the Rudds began the endless preparations for their significant life transition into overseas missions, we traveled on to the Rockies for a short visit with our Crossroads friends, the Gradishar family in Denver. Our families were well matched in age, and we all had a special time together.

The summer passed quickly, with a packed schedule of speaking engagements and meetings. Our various hosts responded with kindness and enthusiasm as we related the contact story and the outcome of my most recent trip to Tanna. Many took advantage of the humor in the story. Michael and Karan Bowsher, Covenant Church summer camp volunteers and owners of a t-shirt business, secretly supplied the entire camp staff with custom-made "John Frum Fan Club" shirts! They all surprised me at our last meal, wearing their new uniforms.

As autumn began, we felt a renewed enthusiasm from the encouragement of our many friends and supporters. Our hearts were back in New Zealand as we prepared for our scheduled trip to Europe in November and wondered what God would do in our brief time of ministry there. We prayed about the purpose and emphasis of our visit and asked God for some definition and insight. Little did we know that we were to find that definition in Anchorage, Alaska.

Danny Gallego and his family had worked with us at Mountain Christian Fellowship in Murphys before moving to the Alaskan wilderness, where Danny now served as a teacher and principal of the large Abbott Loop Christian School. Danny was the one who had "accidentally" given the new-song scriptures from Isaiah to me in 1984. We arrived in Anchorage and enjoyed a warm reunion in the chilly Alaskan autumn.

In the midst of our fellowship and speaking invitations, Shari and I strolled one afternoon through a local shopping mall. Our attention was caught as we both noticed an arresting image at the back of a small art gallery. We had never had much interest in fine art, but as we approached the vigorous impressionist painting, we were both taken with its beauty and power. I was puzzled to see "Vincent" written in the lower left corner. Certainly this was not an original Van Gogh hanging in a mall shop in Anchorage.

I asked the clerk about the painting. She explained that the painting and its frame were a high-tech three-dimensional reproduction of the original "Lilac Bushes" on display at the Hermitage Museum in St. Petersburg, Russia. This laser-created oil-on-canvas copy had faithfully conveyed the texture and color of its creator.

Over the next month, God used this colorful image to lead us into a study of Van Gogh's life. As we learned about his religious background, his painful attempts to make peace with God and with himself and his attempt to worship God through his art, we began to see into the heart of a post-Christian Europe. Everywhere there are the relics of a forgotten faith. The old churches dwarf the individuals as they enter the dark, cold, stony interiors. Vast rooms that were once warmed with the presence of hundreds of the faithful are now lonely and silent. Through our newfound fascination with Van Gogh, we had acquired a burden for the secular European. In a most unexpected way, God had given us the direction and education that we had requested.

Our three major destinations, London, Amsterdam and the South of France, were all places where Van Gogh had lived and painted. We knew that our short time in Europe would bring us opportunities to minister and to visit friends, old and new, but God urged us to make our visit a pilgrimage of prayer for the continent, that God would breathe new life into hollow forms of faith.

Leaving our children in California with Bart and Tina, Shari and I traveled east through Michigan, Ohio and Pennsylvania, visiting friends and relatives before boarding our flight to London.

The immense sea of yellow sodium street lamps seemed to extend in hundreds of ribbons to the horizon as we made our early-morning approach to Heathrow airport. The sheer size of this city, filled with both history and traffic and containing several times the population of New Zealand, was a culture shock. We were relieved to see Jane Harris, who had come to collect us at the airport and take us to a friend's top-floor flat near Earl's Court. Jane, a former *Ruby* officer who had successfully navigated the ship through many a dangerous passage, was in her element as she nudged and wrangled her way through the impeding gridlock of narrow, centuries-old carriageways now straining to handle a modern mobile population.

After recovering from our jet lag, Shari and I emerged from the row house, said our prayers and set out armed with a map of the London Underground Railway as our only hope of survival.

During our stay in London, we had many opportunities to speak with skeptics who were genuinely surprised to hear about the hope of a living Christianity. Often they would astutely question why so much pain and struggle have been a part of the history of the Church. We answered simply that men have always been inclined to do things in defense of their dogma that Jesus would never do. That is why it was important for Jesus to come to us, to show us how to live. I felt like I was giving the same answer that I had given to Isaak One so far away, in another world. Christianity is the only great monotheistic faith that claims that God became man. It is the meekness, peace and power of His life that should be our focus as Christians. Christianity deals with real issues of right and wrong, good and evil, but our dogmatics should always be subordinate to the example and humility of Jesus' life.

Before leaving London, Jane gave us the grand sightseeing tour of the city. She pointed out her fellowship, St. Barnabas Anglican Church, and encouraged us with reports of the life and depth of worship that are being revived among many of God's people. I thought of my own country and its desperate need for religious renewal. In past decades, Britain and America have been driving forces in missions, sending out Christian missionaries all over the world. But now Christians from many developing nations, once targeted by Western missionaries, are mobilizing to evangelize America and England. The tide is turning.

Catherine Matral and her daughter Annabelle were our hosts in Provence, France. Catherine had been a foreign exchange student to my California high school, and we had become friends during that year so long ago. She had watched as I became a Christian and had noted the changes in my life in that first year. She was full of questions about my faith as though we had been apart for only a short time instead of more than two decades.

When Shari and I walked the village streets of Provence in Southern France, we were about as far away from New Zealand as one can get. We looked with wonder at the gardens at St. Remy and thought about how the troubled soul of Van Gogh had come to this place to seek peace and to paint. This monastery had served as Van Gogh's asylum during his bouts with depression. It was here he had created so many of his paintings, including the image we had seen in the Anchorage shop.

Often our hearts were heavy and prayerful as we saw the ruins of millennium-old houses of worship that were once the center of life here. Coming face-to-face with the hopelessness of this faithless place renewed our sense of mission. Our goals and tasks seemed to become clearer and less cluttered. We prayed with greater depth for God to renew hope here.

Near to St. Remy are the recently excavated and partially restored ruins of Glanum, which dates back to the age of the New Testament and beyond. It was fascinating to walk the superbly engineered streets and see the stones laid with exacting precision. The places of worship, sacred pools and many altars, with their inscriptions "TO HERCULES," "TO AGRIPPA" and others, brought to mind the story of Paul in Athens when he noticed the altar "TO AGNOSTO," to an unknown god. That altar was erected by desperate Athenians who had exhausted all their known deities in an effort to end a deadly plague. In humility, the Athenians had acknowledged their ignorance of the one God who could save them, and they cried out to this unknown deity.

God sent Paul, after waiting for decades, to the Athenians to explain who their unknown Savior was— "Jesus Christ, in whom we live and move and have our being." In the many cultures of the world, God has left keys to truth that He sovereignly reveals in His perfect timing. The altar of Athens and the red cross of Tanna, though they are two thousand years and a world apart, bear witness to the same great God, a God who loved us so much that He became man to show us the way and to rescue all people from hopelessness and death.

We had traveled so far in hope of finding something new, only to come full circle and rediscover the universality of the Christian message. Our journey was over. We were coming home.

TWENTY

"As in the Beginning"

OUR whirlwind ministry journey halfway around the world had brought our family back to New Zealand. We had moved back into our home and were slowly unpacking our lives. Pastor Graeme Lauridsen filled me in on the status of the Bay Christian Life Centres. The Papamoa fellowship was thriving and planning to start yet another church farther south in Te Puke. The Mt. Maunganui church was growing under Pastor Graeme's capable leadership, but he and Sharon were feeling led to move to New Zealand's South Island to pastor a church in the city of Dunedin. Therefore I would be needed to assume the senior pastoral role at the Mount church until a permanent replacement could be found. Shari and I considered this request and ultimately felt it would be a good decision.

I was soon back in contact with the pastors on Tanna. In spite of their positive reports of John Frum people coming to Jesus like never before, I was still uneasy, even skeptical, about my strange relationship with these people. God had so clearly burdened us to return to the

Pacific to follow up the work being done here, but I was unsure of my appropriate role in the whole drama. It had been some time since my last visit, and I wondered how things were going for my friends on Tanna. Regardless of my doubts and fears, my desire to make another visit was growing.

I met with Pastor Graeme and Pastor Chris Haines from the local Baptist church and expressed my mixed feelings on my role and relationship with the people and efforts in Tanna. As they lifted me up in prayer, they both strongly exhorted me not to let the curious aspects of my involvement in Tanna keep me from understanding the reality of God's providence in the whole matter. They reassured me that although it might be difficult for me to see, it was clear to them that this was a divinely orchestrated contact and that I should not be timid to speak of the event in those terms. I pondered their words as I began the preparations for my third visit to Vanuatu.

In June 1995, as winter arrived in New Zealand, I found myself in the shop in Port Vila, Vanuatu, debating about the purchase of the curious carving of the man with the bird on his head. I saw myself in the carving, an otherwise all too normal and frail man with a curious and unintended passenger, a prominent feature and identity that was out of my view and understanding yet seemingly clear to others.

I wanted to purchase the figure because of what it humorously symbolized for me. But I hesitated to buy it because to do so seemed, if only to me, to be an act of admission that my role here was more than an amusing South Pacific experience but in fact a stewardship from God. I still wrestled in my heart with accepting the whole affair as a divinely orchestrated appointment with all the responsibility that goes with it. If the bird was no longer on my head, if it had never really been there to begin with, then I was under no special obligations. Our lives could go on back home in the USA or in Europe or wherever. The episode could be filed away as another unusual story, nothing more. I had plenty of ministry responsibility in my life, and I was not looking for any more. Often, I longed for less.

I decided to leave the decision about the "birdman" purchase until after my return from Tanna. By then, God could bring someone else to buy the expensive carving. I would save my money and wait to see how things went on Tanna.

As the small plane began its approach to the rolling grass runway on Tanna, I was pleased to see the very new, bright blue corrugated steel roof that now covered the Lenakel New Life Assembly. We had raised a modest gift from our supporters and church to help defray the cost of materials for the project, and it was a great blessing to see how people's generosity had made such a difference. The Tannese are hard-working, diligent people and had taken the initiative to raise the remainder of the funds in a variety of ways to complete their large house of worship.

As soon as I had collected my baggage and the two boxes of gifts I had brought with me, Pastor Nathan took me to see the church at ground level. I shared the people's excitement as Pastor Nathan and others showed me the covered timber roof structure and the many smart rows of benches. The raised platform was adorned with beautiful fresh flowers and woven garlands. I commended the people on their hard work and complimented the beauty of their sanctuary. I encouraged them to finish reinforcement of one of the structural timbers and asked why a small, perpendicular part of the roof was yet unfinished. They explained that they were unable to connect the two roof lines. I smiled as I thought about the times when, in my early years as a carpenter, I had wrestled with the same confusion about what builders call "hips and valleys." Huts on Tanna have simple straight roofs, and so this feature and its subsequent problem were new to them.

I knelt down over a sandy portion of the ground and with my finger began to draw a solution to the problem. My friends, leaning over to see the picture, expressed continuing confusion at my feeble drawing. My attempts to draw the roof plan with pen on paper met with similar stares. I realized that these able island craftsmen were unacquainted with this kind of two-dimensional representational plan. I pondered for a moment, then tore a page from my notebook. I took out my knife and cut and folded the pieces of paper to form a three-dimensional model of what the roof should look like when finished. The Tannese builders all nodded approval and carefully put the model to work. Soon, they had mastered the new form, and the roof was on its way to completion.

That night was spent in feasting and the exchange of news from our many months of separation. Pastor Nathan presented the latest reports about developments among the John Frum people. His church was leading the effort among Assemblies of God workers and pastors, planting churches in Frum villages and seeing a dramatic influx of Frum people and chiefs since our original visit two years ago. I was particularly encouraged to hear about Chief Isaak's baptism a few months earlier.

"It is only a matter of time now," Nathan said, as he shared about his own personal conversations with Isaak One. "But the chief is in a delicate position, as he is the head of the main John Frum village. There are other Frum leaders who are afraid to lose their power and so put pressure on him to close the doors to the church."

It was clear that Isaak could use some encouragement. I was eager to see him again, but I was uncertain as to what encouragement I could give. Manu, the astute church elder and leader at the Star School, said, "Pastor John, you have to realize that Chief Isaak One is a man who is driven by visions and dreams, by miracles. You have to let him know what a miracle it was for you to come here, how God led you here. You have to stand up for what God has done here, make it plain to him."

I was amazed to hear these words from my Tannese brother, as only days before I had received very similar encouragement from the church leaders in New Zealand. Manu's exhortation was very much in line with the advice from Pastors Graeme and Chris.

In the morning, a truck arrived to take several of us down the black-sand coast along the southwestern side of Tanna and up into the highland bush where the Iakamhau Star School was continuing to thrive. Grinning children ran out to greet us as I put candies into a sea of persistent hands. I encouraged the teachers as we toured their class-rooms and admired the proudly displayed work of their students. I was impressed to see how far these Frum children had progressed in their studies over the past year. I explained to the people how God was send-ing the Rudds to help them acquire curricula, build permanent build-ings and help develop their teaching staff. Pastor Nathan excitedly presented his ideas for more schools in Frum villages where they had recently planted churches. Together we discussed a plan to enable each Frum village to have its own church and school building with their own pastors and teachers.

I learned that the hard-working teachers here had gone for three months without their very minimum wages, but I was heartened to hear that the financial gift I had brought from our supporters and the Mount church would more than make up the difference and enable them to continue their work. I was humbled to see the devotion of these dedicated servants. Taking our leave of the busy teachers and smiling children, we climbed back into our truck.

As we returned to Lenakel, the driver stopped beside the island's petrol station. The small shack was surrounded by large drums of diesel fuel and gasoline. The attendant hand-pumped the fuel into spouted buckets, and the driver carefully poured the precious petroleum into his thirsty tank. As we stood by, Pastor Nathan spotted a man emerging from a truck and said, "There is David Bennett. He is a very good evangelist to John Frum people."

I was happy to meet this tall and fit American. I had corresponded with him and his wife, Marilyn. The Bennetts were working with the Missionary Baptist Church and had left their home and family in California to work in Western Samoa and now in Vanuatu. They shared our burden for evangelism and education. David spent much of his time evangelizing, baptizing and helping build churches and schools in remote John Frum villages. As we shook hands, David was excitedly speaking Bislama. Slowly making the mental transition to talking to another American, he shifted into English and greeted me warmly.

David was unaware of my previous history with John Frum and Isaak One. I took the opportunity to ask him about his experience with John Frum evangelism. He reported that in the past two years, he had seen an unprecedented number of Frum people and chiefs coming to Christ and being baptized. He spoke about the immense needs in the more isolated villages, which he had been the first Westerner to visit. "There are many more Frum people and villages than we have thought!" he stated emphatically.

David went on to say that the road to Sulphur Bay, which used to regularly be filled with pilgrims headed for the John Frum celebrations, held only a trickle now. I rejoiced that the reality of Jesus Christ was having such a dramatic effect on so many Frum people.

Later in the day, I met with Presbyterian pastors James and Willy. Again they spoke about the clear results that our first curious contact had helped to foster. That encounter had opened the door for them to work in Frum villages as never before. The two pastors now had an invitation to put a church near Sulphur Bay. This was quite remarkable, given the history of hostility between the Presbyterian church and the John Frum movement.

The reports were all extremely positive, but I was concerned about Chief Isaak One. It had to be difficult for him to see these changes to his way of life and leadership taking place. I thought that he could probably use some encouragement that the bold decisions he had made were indeed the right ones.

I recalled the advice that Manu and my pastoral leadership in New Zealand had given me to boldly stand for the providence of God in this whole matter. Chief Isaak One was a man driven by dreams and visions and sensitive to the divine fulfillment of his people's expectations. I would have to throw off my Western skepticism about their values and way of life and learn to be more like him. As presumptuous and absurd as the ideas were to me, I had to accept my role in their culture and fulfill my opportunity to encourage the changes that God had sovereignly brought in spite of me. I had to quit questioning God's mysterious methods. After all, how could I decline participation in God's exciting and amazing plans? I had to cease being a subjective critic of these things and complete the divine appointment.

Later that evening as the tropic night quickly fell, the generator was "pull-corded" to life. The droplights in the rafters flickered on, and the amplifier boosted the sounds of praise out from the new Lenakel church and into the bush where cut trails were bringing young people from all over the island. The combined meeting of some five hundred youth and their families and pastors filled the building as various groups came forward, in turn, to present their contribution of special music. As each group left the platform, a deacon stood by to collect the group's offering while the crowd applauded in appreciation.

I spoke simply, through an interpreter, about the power of young people who take a stand for Jesus Christ. Just like the three children in the fiery furnace, these young people would enjoy the special company of Jesus. I returned to my seat, thinking of the many more precious children on this island who would be coming to Christ, learning God's Word and standing up for Jesus. The strength and power of the young people's worship continued into the night long after I had retired. I prayed for wisdom for my next day's visit with Isaak at Sulphur Bay.

The now familiar drive over the central summit and across the barren volcanic landscape afforded me the time to think further about this important visit with my friend, the chief. I thought about how I could explain the meaning of our first meeting in a way that would bind us together in our histories. I thought about the many times I had heard my island friends speak of generations of their history and how they saw the strands all coming together to the present moment, giving it meaning and fulfillment. I wondered how I could describe my history. I took out my wallet and removed a very recent photo. Just before leaving the United States, our family had arranged for a group photo. My brother Bart and I had gathered together with our wives and children, forming a huddle around Mom and Dad. It was the first time we had ever taken such a photo, and I carried one of the smaller copies with me. I had often rejoiced as I viewed the Rush family all together. I remembered the time when I had been the first to come to Christ and had felt so isolated, but now we were all heaven bound, three generations of us. I had my answer.

Chief Isaak One and I sat together with our interpreter under the main meeting shelter in the center of the village. We exchanged our greetings and affirmed our friendship. I presented the photo to the chief. "This is my family back in America," I said. "My father is also named John, like his father before him. He has been sick for a long time. He was an officer in the United States Navy, and he sends his greetings. The tall boy in the picture is my son. He is also named John. I hope that he will be able to come to Tanna one day and meet my friends here in Sulphur Bay.

"I want to tell you about how God sent me here to Tanna," I continued. "I was a pastor in a church in the mountains of California. I knew nothing about Tanna. One day God showed me a vision of a white ship in the Pacific Ocean, and then He changed everything in my life so that I could be aboard that ship. It was a ship that God used to help people in the islands. God sent us to Tanna. He showed us that we would be like John the Baptist and help your people to put their trust in Jesus Christ.

"For many years, you and your people have waited for John Frum America to come on a white ship and bring good things with him. What you have been waiting for has now happened. And now you are working with the church to help your people learn about Jesus. This is a good thing. It is good to work together. We are going to try to send more help and more people in the future. We want to help you. I want to help you."

The chief listened intently to all that I said. When I had finished, he spoke with warm gratitude and assured me of his commitment and desire to continue working with the church. I had brought as a gift a box of clothing from New Zealand Christians. We opened the box, and Isaak removed a t-shirt. The shirt, bearing a message for racial unity in New Zealand, was a powerful, though unintentional message to the chief. It depicted brown and white figures at the base of a bright red cross. The caption was a simple prayer: "Let us all be one." God was at it again. He had providentially supplied another perfect gift. I explained to the chief how Jesus was wanting us to work together as one to bring the gospel to his people.

As we walked along the beach beside the village stockade fence, the chief spoke to Pastor Nathan. "Your grandfather used to give food to my grandfather many years ago. Your grandfather brought the gospel to my grandfather with peace and love. Then the church was cruel to us, and we left. But now you have brought the gospel to us again, with peace and love, as in the beginning."

Pastor Nathan was overjoyed to hear that their histories had once more come together into a single stream. Years ago, John Frum had said that a better religion would one day come to Tanna. His words had indeed come true.

On my way home to New Zealand, I had a brief layover in Port Vila. Returning to the shop, I stared once again at the birdman carving. Thinking of one last consideration, I took the figure to the counter and asked the clerk, "Does this figure have any significance or special meaning here in Vanuatu?"

The woman behind the counter readily responded, "Oh, yes! The man with the bird on his head is the man with the message. He comes from far away, like a bird, and brings the news."

"I'll take it!" I said, without another thought.

TWENTY-ONE

New Song

ELIZABETH, who holds a powerful position as a prophetess for John Frum, has been said to make "a new song every day...about the love and the law of John Frum," and how the people "will live forever when John Frum comes."[1] Seeing her influence dwindle when Chief Isaak One opened his village to Christian missionaries, Elizabeth sternly opposed the growing cooperation between the church and John Frum leaders. But her own words and prophecies, linking the figure of John Frum with the biblical John the Baptist, had unintentionally contributed to the groundwork for the introduction of Jesus Christ into the John Frum culture.

John Frum religion, having its basis in oral tradition alone, is a complex synthesis of folklore, American military custom and Judeo-Christian influences. It is also a revolutionary movement that was successful in breaking the control of the church and the Tanna laws that sought to eradicate the Tannese people's island way of life.

As a result of many influences, John Frum is seen as the reincarnation of Tanna's powerful volcano god, as an American military liberator, as John the Baptist and as much more. Even his name has a variety of spellings and interpretations. There is no way to simplify the vast number of Frum legends that have come orally through a number of isolated times, villages and visionary experiences. Mythology defies systematic analysis.

I am commonly asked, "Who is John Frum? Where did he come from? Did he ever exist? What about his long-awaited return?"

In my view, John Frum is a redemptive analogy that God placed within this people group to be fulfilled at the proper time with the revelation of Jesus Christ. Don Richardson's book *Eternity in Their Hearts* presents a number of accounts wherein remote and isolated peoples have been prepared for the gospel by a prediction in their own folk culture about the coming of a man with a special book or a different color of skin, or by a predisposition to monotheistic worship. *Operation World*, a definitive and comprehensive prayer and missions handbook, lists the Vanuatu cargo cults as unevangelized people groups. My first antagonistic reply from Chief Isaak One, when he denied any interest in Jesus Christ or the church, certainly bore this out. Yet there were clear links in the Tannese people's own belief system not only to an American named John but also to Christianity.

Now, only three years after the Mercy Ships outreach to John Frum people at Sulphur Bay, local pastors and evangelists report, "John Frum is finished." They tell the story of how Frum chiefs and villagers are coming to Christ. Even Elizabeth, the John Frum prophetess, is now attending services and no longer opposing the work of the church.

I personally believe that John Frum was originally an American Christian visiting or living in Tanna in the early 1930s. John Frum was troubled by the way in which the church leaders were, without seeking to understand the island customs, suppressing the way of life of his native friends. He tried to encourage these friends with some of the earliest statements attributed to John Frum that "the church is good, the Bible is good, but your customs are also good." With or without knowing it, he was adding powerful religious fuel to the growing discontent. These words prompted the Tannese to violate the laws forbidding their traditional customs, and in a misguided effort to control the movement, the church reacted with cruel suppression.

By this time, perhaps with a promise to return, John Frum had left Tanna and was unable to give further guidance to his friends. Reports about his appearances became more mystical, and his statements took on a defiant tone. In the face of the cruelty, the now phantomlike John tells the Tannese people that the church is bad and they are to leave it and take their children out of the church-run schools. One day a better religion would come to Tanna, but for now the people are to return to their native ways and abandon the church.

These beliefs led to the island's unified rejection of the church, to the extreme of nailing the doors shut, leaving other doors wide open and eventually resulting in the adoption of the U.S. military "religion" and customs. As the cargo cult grew and developed, the figure of John Frum remained central. In his absence, the variety of stories regarding his return emerged, including the interesting version of Frum's return on a white ship bringing medical and other help.

By God's design, we sailed into this historical and mythical context in May 1993, arousing these complex expectations. Our only preparation for the contact had been the clear emphasis of our prayer groups on the person and work of John the Baptist, the "John" who courageously encouraged his own faithful followers to leave him and devote themselves to Jesus. In many ways, this is the vital role of John Frum as well. As in Jesus' day, not all followers will be able to make the transition, especially those who, as in New Testament times, expected their deliverance to be material and political. But in the course of time, Jesus will be seen by many to be the spiritual liberator that they have long awaited.

The question is often asked, "Are you John Frum?" To this I will say that the mythical and redemptive figure of John Frum is much larger than any of the individual ideas and personalities that have played a role in this work. To the degree that the individual facets have moved the Frum people toward a renewed faith in Jesus Christ, they have been true to the divine and redemptive purpose that Frum is meant to play.

At the very least, I believe that the many remarkable consequences of our visit in May 1993 provided the perfect opportunity for Chief Isaak One and other John Frum leaders and people, already longing for change, to be reconciled with their Tannese neighbors and the church and to realize the benefits of education and the improved life that they felt would come with it. At the other interpretive extreme, our arrival was, in fact, the fulfillment of a redemptive key placed within the John Frum people at a time appointed by a sovereign and loving God who will go to extraordinary lengths to draw all people to Himself.

On a purely secular plane, Leonard Nimoy, anxious to distance himself from the powerful *Star Trek* myth that was building around him, wrote the 1975 autobiographical cry, *I Am Not Spock.* Now after thirty years of continuing popularity of the original pointy-eared Vulcan character, Nimoy has found it impossible to distinguish himself from the legend and so says with sane resignation, "Maybe I am Spock after all."[2] I can understand Nimoy's confusion and resignation. Maybe I am John Frum after all. Maybe not. Such is the nature of myth.

It must be said, however, before we children of the West are critical of such folk expectations, that we are the epitome of cargo cults. We have recklessly pursued our technology and comforts in a futile and world-ravaging hope for happiness and fulfillment. In our growing spiritual and moral vacuum, we are the ones obsessed with "cargo" and the rituals of status and materialism. If we are true to these rituals, if we obtain more "cargo," we believe that fulfillment will come. The Tannese have simply tried to imitate our empty forms. The only hope for all cargo people, from remote village to city high-rise, is a life-changing relationship with Jesus Christ. The Frum people are now embracing that reality, but are we?

Predicting a dismal future for the John Frum people, the author of the 1974 *National Geographic* article wrote, "And so cultists cling to Frum in hopes of a better life, while Western critics see the movement marching a downhill road to unfulfilled promises and inevitable disappointment."[3] He neglected to take into account the never-tiring love of an omniscient God who was even then preparing the way for His truth to utterly fulfill every promise and hope of the fascinating John Frum people.

Afterword

THIS book has largely been about the authors' three-year effort to more fully understand the expectation of the John Frum people and John's place within their world. It has also been about the increasingly successful local efforts to reach these people for Christ and how this grassroots Tannese effort can best be supported. Truly, this book's story is still being written, and new chapters in the history of the John Frum people are being added continually.

Every day, more John Frum leaders and villagers are making the choice to follow Jesus Christ and become a part of the indigenous church in Tanna. The Tannese church is working diligently and across denominational lines to meet the spiritual and educational needs of these people and their villages. The magnitude of these new demands is beyond the resources of their impoverished population, and therefore vital opportunities exist for individuals, churches and organizations to help these dedicated Tannese national workers.

Motivated by the words in Isaiah 42:10, New Song has worked for five years to assist in the development of helpful projects among the John Frum people and in Vanuatu. In this time we have been encouraged to see the planting of several churches, twenty schools and four teacher-training programs in Port Vila and on Tanna. We are most excited to see how readily the Vanuatu nationals master and carry out the work of ministry to the needs around them. Their dedication and hard work inspire us.

We are grateful for the support of a variety of denominational churches and individuals in New Zealand, Vanuatu and the United States who have provided funding, short- and long-term workers and construction teams. New Zealand and U.S. schools have provided thousands of textbooks, computers, furnishings and other supplies. Special gratitude is to be extended to David Bennett, Salt Lake Christian Fellowship, Kevin Ahern and the leaders of the New Zealand Assemblies of God who have been very kind to give us frequent coverage in the *Evangel* magazine as well as to provide accounting and promotional help. We are very grateful to God for the help of so many people who have allowed us to reach and serve the John Frum people and for the many other organizations that are doing so much.

If you desire to help with these ongoing efforts, or if you would like to arrange for John Rush to speak for your church, organization, conference or training school, please contact New Song today or check our website for current information:

New Song Information
P.O. Box 2578
Murphys, CA 95247
USA
TEL: 1 (800) 748–SONG
EMAIL: NewsongINF@aol.com
WEBSITE: www.johnfrum.com

In addition, countless opportunities are available for volunteer service worldwide with YWAM and Mercy Ships. If you are interested in short- or long-term service, you can obtain information by writing or calling

Mercy Ships — International
P.O. Box 2020
Lindale, TX 75771-2020
USA
1 (800) 424–SHIP

Endnotes

Chapter 4

1. Oliver E. Allen et al., *The Pacific Navigators* (Alexandria, Virginia: Time-Life Books, 1980), p. 156.
2. Edward Rice, *John Frum He Come* (New York: Doubleday and Co., 1974), p. 187.
3. Juniper Films in association with The Discovery Channel, *Pacifica: The Fiery Messiah*, 1993.
4. Rice, *John Frum He Come*, p. 192.
5. Ibid., p. 175.
6. Ibid., p. 198.
7. Ibid., p. 91.
8. *Vanuatu: Discover Our Islands* (Port Vila: Vanuatu Institute of Technology, 1981), p. 180, quoted in Lamont Lindstrom, *Cargo Cults: Strange Stories of Desire from Melanesia and Beyond* (Honolulu: University of Hawaii Press, 1993), p. 132.

Chapter 6

1. "Glory, Glory Lord." Words and music by Bob Fitts. © 1990 Scripture in Song. Adm. Maranatha! Music c/o The Copyright Co., 40 Music Square East, Nashville, TN 37203.
2. "Lord, I Lift Your Name on High." Words and music by Rick Founds. © 1989 Maranatha! Music. Adm. by The Copyright Co., 40 Music Square East, Nashville, TN 37203.

Chapter 9

1. Stephen Jay Gould, "Is a New and General Theory of Evolution Emerging?" *Paleobiology*, Vol. 6 (January 1980), p. 127.

Chapter 13

1. "Glory, Glory Lord." Words and music by Bob Fitts. © 1990 Scripture in Song. Adm. Maranatha! Music c/o The Copyright Co., 40 Music Square East, Nashville, TN 37203.

Chapter 21

1. Juniper Films in association with The Discovery Channel, *Pacifica: The Fiery Messiah*, 1993.
2. Divina Infusino, "Out of Character—Nimoy," *Star Trek: Special Edition, TV Guide* (Spring 1995), p. 53.
3. Kal Muller, "Tanna Awaits the Coming of John Frum," *National Geographic* (May 1974), p. 714.

Dominating the island terrain, Yasur, one of the world's most accessible volcanoes, rumbles forbiddingly over Lake Siwi and the villages below.

The Lenakel open-air market: selling fruits and vegetables beneath a giant banyan tree.

In the distance, the Ruby lies safely at anchor, away from the treacherous coral outcroppings where village boys spear fish and play.

(right and below)
The Ruby's arrival in Tanna in May 1993 piqued the interest of local cargo cult members, who had been waiting patiently for fifty years for the arrival of a white ship bringing a man named John from America with the answers to their problems.

(right and facing top)
John Rush conducts a conference for island ministers and finds himself at the center of island prophecies.

Red-tipped bamboo "bayonet rifles" stand in the corner of the John Frum headquarters—a shrine filled with mementos and relics from WWII and posters proclaiming the movement's dedication to America and the coming of "John Frum."

(left) An unpretentious man known for his no-nonsense style and devotion to John Frum, Chief Isaak One is an influential island leader of over 10,000 people.

(right) John Rush meets the John Frum chief in a traditional hand-shaking ceremony.

Under the shadow of their sacred volcano, Chief Isaak One leads a welcoming party along a freshly garlanded pathway prepared especially for the arrival of the Ruby's team.

The revered symbol of the John Frum movement is the medic's red cross. For over half a century, it has represented not Christianity but the hope of the John Frum people that one day "America" would come back to save them.

(right and facing) John Frum villagers gather to hear the message from the Mercy Ship's team.

Singing hymns of devotion to America, the villagers escort their guests ceremoniously through the village.

Amidst great ceremony and anticipation, ship director John Rush and fellow crew members arrive in Sulphur Bay.

(left and facing)
Pastor John shares the message, "We cannot wait for America to help us. We have to put our hope and trust in Jesus Christ."

A young English-speaking girl reads a letter of request from the chief.

Beneath the proudly displayed flags, the chiefs retreat into the John Frum headquarters to meet with ship representatives.

Pastor Willy, Gary Peters, John Rush, Chief Isaak One, Pastor James, and a John Frum interpreter near the ashen slopes of Yasur volcano.

Within the stockade-style fence, Chief Isaak One greets Gary Peters, a member of the Ruby's *crew and a U.S. Navy veteran.*

A parting gift to the crew—a seven-foot boat fashioned out of fruit in the shape of the Pacific Ruby.

The new roof of the almost completed Assembly of God church in Lenakel, made possible by donations made through New Song Ministries.

Jack Rudd with the Executive Council of the Vanuatu Assemblies of God, Port Vila, June 1995

(left and below) *The children of the newly opened Iakamhau Star School are among the first of the John Frum people to receive an education.*

A young teacher instructs eager pupils at Iakamhau Star School.

A simple Tannese kitchen.

Basket weaving: Life on Tanna has remained virtually unchanged over the years and revolves around everyday family activities.

Christian Heroes: Then & Now

Adventure-filled Christian biographies for ages 10 to 100!

Readers of all ages love the exciting, challenging, and deeply touching true stories of ordinary men and women whose trust in God accomplished extraordinary exploits for His kingdom and glory.

Gladys Aylward: The Adventure of a Lifetime • 1-57658-019-9
Nate Saint: On a Wing and a Prayer • 1-57658-017-2
Hudson Taylor: Deep in the Heart of China • 1-57658-016-4
Amy Carmichael: Rescuer of Precious Gems • 1-57658-018-0
Eric Liddell: Something Greater Than Gold • 1-57658-137-3
Corrie ten Boom: Keeper of the Angels' Den • 1-57658-136-5
William Carey: Obliged to Go • 1-57658-147-0
George Müller: The Guardian of Bristol's Orphans • 1-57658-145-4
Jim Elliot: One Great Purpose • 1-57658-146-2
Mary Slessor: Forward into Calabar • 1-57658-148-9
David Livingstone: Africa's Trailblazer • 1-57658-153-5
Betty Greene: Wings to Serve • 1-57658-152-7
Adoniram Judson: Bound for Burma • 1-57658-161-6
Cameron Townsend: Good News in Every Language • 1-57658-164-0
Jonathan Goforth: An Open Door in China • 1-57658-174-8
Lottie Moon: Giving Her All for China • 1-57658-188-8
John Williams: Messenger of Peace • 1-57658-256-6
William Booth: Soup, Soap, and Salvation • 1-57658-258-2
Rowland Bingham: Into Africa's Interior • 1-57658-282-5
Ida Scudder: Healing Bodies, Touching Hearts • 1-57658-285-X
Wilfred Grenfell: Fisher of Men • 1-57658-292-2
Lillian Trasher: The Greatest Wonder in Egypt • 1-57658-305-8
Loren Cunningham: Into All the World • 1-57658-199-3
Florence Young: Mission Accomplished • 1-57658-313-9
Sundar Singh: Footprints Over the Mountains • 1-57658-318-X
C.T. Studd: No Retreat • 1-57658-288-4
Rachel Saint: A Star in the Jungle • 1-57658-337-6
Brother Andrew: God's Secret Agent • 1-57658-355-4
Count Zinzendorf: Firstfruit • 1-57658-262-0
Clarence Jones: Mr. Radio • 1-57658-343-0

Available from YWAM Publishing
1-800-922-2143
www.ywampublishing.com
Also available: Christian Heroes Unit Study Curriculum Guides